MAR 2 0 2002

ORIGINAL YOUTH

THE REAL STORY OF

EDMUND WHITE'S BOYHOOD

ORIGINAL YOUTH

THE REAL STORY OF

EDMUND WHITE'S BOYHOOD

KEITH FLEMING
WITH AN INTRODUCTION BY DAVID LEAVITT

GREEN
CANDY
PRESS

Original Youth: The Real Story of Edmund White's Boyhood
by Keith Fleming
ISBN 1-931160-20-1
Published by Green Candy Press
www.greencandypress.com

Grateful acknowledgment is made for permission to quote from the
following works:

From *Nocturnes for the King of Naples* by Edmund White, copyright © 1978 by
Edmund White. St. Martin's Press

From *A Boy's Own Story* by Edmund White, copyright © 1982 by Edmund
White. Used by permission of Dutton, a division of Penguin Group (USA) Inc.

From *States of Desire* by Edmund White, copyright © 1983 by Edmund White.
Used by permission of Edmund White

From *Forgetting Elena* by Edmund White, copyright © 1990 by Edmund
White. Ballantine, a division of Random House, Inc.

From *Skinned Alive: Stories* by Edmund White, copyright © 1995 by Edmund
White. Alfred A. Knopf, a division of Random House, Inc.

From *The Beautiful Room is Empty* by Edmund White, copyright © 1998 by
Edmund White. Used by permission of Alfred A. Knopf, a division of Random
House, Inc.

Printed in Canada by Transcontinental
Massively Distributed by P.G.W.

For Mari, Murdoch, and Margaret

Acknowledgments

I'd like to thank Don Daskais, Sue White, Jean White Snow, George Newman, Marilyn Schaefer, Johanna Tabin, Steve Turner, Thomas McGuane, Ray Sakolov, Fred Mitchell, John Hunting, Patrick Merla, Stanley Redfern, Keith McDermott, Michael Denneny, Jeffrey Welch, Patricia Willis at the Beinecke Library at Yale University, Andrew McBeth and Kevin Bentley at Green Candy, and Delilah White, Penny McLeod, and Helen White in memory. And of course Margaret Fleming and Edmund White. Some proper names and identifying details have been changed to protect the privacy of living individuals.

Contents

૨૯

Preface

Edmund White, now so closely associated with gay liberation, gay subculture, and the 1970s promiscuity he chronicled in his auto-biographical novel *The Farewell Symphony*, spent many years and thousands of dollars trying to go straight. Though he participated in the Stonewall Uprising, it was not until several years later, after he'd already become a gay spokesman and leader, that he was able to reach a full acceptance of his homosexuality. It's no wonder that his writing has always displayed an uncanny knack for identifying and untangling human contradictions. Or that he himself, on every level, has been a walking bundle of contradictions all his life: someone warmly feeling yet coldly observing who, to list just a few more examples, is ceaselessly sexual yet always more concerned with the pleasure of others; tirelessly sociable yet, inside himself, at a "Buddhist remove" from the world; bleakly cynical and yet buoyant and full of life.

As a boy his contradictions were already so intricate that the interplay in him between guilt and desire, boldness and self-denial, bragging and betrayal requires careful explanation to be fully understood. Even as a small child he was wily and complex enough to be misread by everyone around him, and by the time he was a teenager the central focus of his life had become his intensely contradictory existence as an unwilling, secretive, but nonetheless very active and "possessed" young homosexual. These contradictions and habits of mind are all a part of what I consider to be the "originality" of his youth. Certainly the story of Edmund White's young life offers many glimpses into the formation of a distinctive and fascinating personality. But his story also shows him to be an almost eerie representative of a whole gay genera-tion's feelings—the only difference being that Ed White felt all these feelings to an extreme and usually acted on them, sometimes to a sensational extent.

Though I've known my "Uncle Ed" all my life and first got close to him as a teenager while living with him in New York (a story told in my memoir *The Boy with the Thorn in His Side*), the full dimensions of Edmund White's youth are something I only began to grasp when I began delving into the subject in earnest. Growing up I'd often heard bits and pieces about Ed's youth from my mother, Margaret, his older sister, who would recall the weird and colorful days when she, Ed, and their mother Delilah lived in tiny quarters at a luxury hotel in suburban Chicago following "their" divorce from E.V. White, Ed's father (the divorce was spoken of as something E.V. had done to the three of them, as in "Daddy divorced us"). From Delilah, my grandmother, I'd heard how strangely poised and brilliant "Eddie" had been as a little boy—so much so that, characteristically putting her own self-glorifying spin on things, Delilah said she'd often been tempted to write a book called *How to Raise a Genius*.

When I began interviewing Ed over the phone he was living in Paris and I discovered that the time to reach him was in the morning. At that hour he'd be at his best—fresh, focused, will-ing—his enthusiasm not yet depleted by his exhausting daily round of socializing. Often he'd be deeply relaxed and expansive, and occasionally I'd hear a discreet splash in the background and realize he was talking to me from his bathtub!

But it was more than the morning hour that made these inter-views so special. In retrospect I can see how unusually open and available Ed happened to be during those early months of 1995. His lover Hubert Sorin (a central figure in the novel *The Married Man*) had died of AIDS the previous spring, and Ed hadn't yet met his current partner, Michael Carroll. Live-in lovers are essential for Ed's emotional well-being and he would sometimes complain to me that for all the dinner parties he gave and attended, he'd always find himself alone again and lonely at the end of the evening. In early 1995 he also had the feeling he was living out his final days. He'd been diagnosed HIV positive in 1985 and in his new emptiness he'd begun to suspect that his own number must be due to come up soon; worse, he was beset with a sense of "living posthumously," of having outlived his friends and lovers. It was a terrible way to feel, and yet it made him an ideal interviewee. Ordinarily Ed is always a bit distracted by having his fingers in so many pies, but during the extraordinary time of my interviews with him he became as pensive and fond of probing and coming to grips with the past as someone making a final confession.

There's no escaping the embarrassing precision with which the young Edmund White's relationships with his parents adhere to the old Freudian recipe for making a son gay: take one distant, scary father, one overwhelming mother, one impressionable boy, and bake until gay. In fact, when Ed published his novel *Nocturnes for the King of Naples*, which contained semiautobiographical passages about him and his parents, one exasperated gay critic charged him with undermining the greater cause of gay liberation by validating the notion that homosexuality is a by-product of warped parenting. And yet for all this I've become convinced by the particulars of Ed's youth that he was very much born and not bred gay. One of his earliest memories is of sitting in the lap of an Air Force pilot as a four-year-old boy and wanting to stay in this man's lap because he liked the smell of him, his voice, his warmth.

I would even argue that Ed's having been such a mama's boy was something that fed off his homosexuality, rather than created it. His most incestuous-seeming acts as a boy with his mother— giving her long back rubs while she lay drunkenly in bed, sleeping in the same bed with her, helping her button up her "Merry Widow" girdle—are precisely the kinds of things a heterosexual son would have found too sexually charged to perform. In other words, to sleep in the same bed with Delilah would be quite a loaded experience for a straight son, but for a boy inherently gay it's not nearly so big a deal. Margaret, my mother, who's been a practicing lesbian for the past quarter century and who recognizes now that she was gay all along, remembers *not* wanting to help Delilah in and out of her Merry Widow because, as a "proto-lesbian" daughter, it would have been too emotionally and sexually overwhelming.

My mother functioned as the perfect inside counter-source to Ed himself. Our family has a natural confessional bent, and Margaret and Ed each took candor to new heights in their interviews with me, offering up the past in hilarious, shocking, embarrassing detail. But there are limits even to Ed's candor (as well as to his memory of the distant past), and Margaret was the one who told me about often coming home late in the evening as a high school student to find Ed and Delilah asleep in the same bed. Margaret's memory is so astonishingly vivid that Ed consulted her himself while writing his novel about his youth, *A Boy's Own Story*. And yet—interestingly—*A Boy's Own Story*, which cemented Edmund White's literary reputation and is still perhaps his best-known book, is the work of "autofiction," as he calls his autobiographical fiction, in which he departs most from real life (the later installments of his fictional autobiography, *The Beautiful Room Is Empty* and *The Farewell Symphony*, have grown progressively truer to life).

Many of the changes and omissions in *Boy's Own* were part of a deliberate scheme to make his literary stand-in more "universal" and sympathetic to readers by toning down how actively homosexual he'd been as a boy. There is no mention in the novel, for instance, of the regular sex he began having at thirteen with adult men he picked up at a train station men's room. Nor is there any mention of just how cultivated he was from very early on. For along with censoring most of his teenage sex, Ed also withheld from *Boy's Own* his own story as an aspiring writer and there is thus no mention of the two novels he wrote in prep school, *Dark Currents* and *Mrs. Morrigan*, or of the key role his poetry played in winning him his first real friends. (Interestingly, a strong argument can be made that Ed had no real interest in social life until his sex drive had kicked in with puberty.) *A Boy's Own Story* also minimizes the least attractive theme in Ed's youth: his betrayals. This perverse impulse to betray people, rooted in his parents' own "double betrayal" of him as a little boy, was very much a part of the twisted resentments and self-hatred he acquired as a gay teen living in the intensely homophobic middle America of the 1950s.

In these pages fact and fiction have been painstakingly sorted out and new material has brought to light intriguing aspects of Ed's actual boyhood that have never been written about or, in some instances, even known. While writing this very intimate account I came to see Ed's youth as being, at its heart, an inner drama: the story of a boy who made a habit of keeping the most compelling aspects of his life secret. None of his friends at the time suspected the extent or even the existence of the war going on within him regarding his sexuality. From the beginning, it seems, he was adept at projecting a quite different person from the complicated one he was on the inside.

Introduction

by David Leavitt

When I was in my early twenties and living in New York, two figures defined the so-called "gay literary scene": Larry Kramer and Edmund White. I had not yet met either one of them; each existed for me as book and myth. Kramer was a polemicist, a troublemaker, best known for his satirical novel *Faggots*, in which he not only skewered the self-indulgent culture of 1970s gay New York, but prophesied its collapse in an ash-heap of horror. White, on the other hand, was the consummate literary novelist, author of such rarefied books as *Forgetting Elena* and *Nocturnes for the King of Naples*. He lived in Paris, remotely and (I presumed) glamorously, while Kramer lived on lower Fifth Avenue and had his number in the phone book. Both seemed to engender controversy—albeit very different sorts of controversy—whatever they did. White followed the immensely influential *A Boy's Own Story* with *Caracole*, a fanciful roman à clef that provoked a minor earthquake in literary New York, as well as an irreparable breach between him and his onetime champions, Susan Sontag and Richard Howard. Meanwhile Kramer was co-founding the Gay Men's Health Crisis as well as ACT-UP! (the AIDS Coalition to Unleash Power), irritating the mayor and a lot of rich people with his diatribes, and writing the first AIDS play, *The Normal Heart*. Even today these two men embody opposite poles of the literary compass: Kramer the activist, for whom literature exists, above all else, to serve political ends, and White the artist, for whom the idea of literature serving anything but itself is repugnant.

An attack Kramer made a few years back on White's novel *The Farewell Symphony* exemplified the schism. For Kramer, *The*

Farewell Symphony was an evil book because it described unapolo-
getically the erotic petri dish in which, during the 1970s, the HIV
virus evolved. In other words, it did not serve the proper goal: dis-
couraging the phoenix-like revival of pre-AIDS gay culture by
arguing for that culture's immorality. For White, on the contrary,
The Farewell Symphony was, very simply, a novel, and as such
answerable only to itself; as Oscar Wilde once memorably put it,
"There is no such thing as a moral or an immoral book. Books are
well written, or badly written. That is all." This was a position
with which I personally agreed. At the same time, it was hard to
dismiss Kramer's claim that gay literature, by the end of the twen-
tieth century, had become almost obsessively preoccupied with
sexual detail (and in particular sexual fantasy), as well as his terror at the abandonment of safe sex practices by young gay men
around the world.

So preoccupied was Kramer with ideology, so determined to
draft literature into the service of politics, that he failed to recognize or appreciate just what was wonderful about *The Farewell
Symphony*: the writing. Whether hymning a long-lost young
man's New York, or eulogizing a dead poet, or focusing in on the
small, sometimes ugly details that demystify and humanize most
sexual encounters, White exhibited the artist's natural flair and
his allergy to piety. I remember with particular vividness a
hilarious moment in *The Farewell Symphony* when one character
asks another to shit on him, and is disappointed when his lover
provides only a little "ètron." Sex, in this scene, provides an
opportunity for White to articulate the odd pathos that so often
accompanies the enactment of a "hard" erotic fantasy. His is the
light touch of the serious artist, not the sledgehammer blow of
the zealot.

Most of White's stories are likewise rooted in autobiography,
and make no pretense to be otherwise; in "His Biographer," the
complex ethics of turning a lived life into a told narrative even
becomes the subject. Yet the majority of the stories are really about
love and grief, as they are experienced over a long span of years. In
all of them, posing questions proves to be of greater importance
than answering them—yet another way in which White's work

fails the test of polemic. Nor is any detail deemed too sacred or too unholy to merit inclusion. Instead details are given emphasis for one reason only—because they help in the task of moving the story forward; because they tell.

White has sometimes been accused of being a cold writer, and while a certain observational chilliness does occasionally bring down the temperature of his work, more often than not, narrative distance achieves the paradoxical goal of making them seem more immediate, more intimate. Nor is the narrator, the writer figure, ever allowed to take a position of moral superiority to the people he encounters; indeed, the coldness may be a necessary consequence of White's effort to write about himself as if he were someone else. (Paradoxically, in White's warmest book, *The Married Man*, he writes about himself in the third person.) And even that effort is secondary to the larger goal of creating a compelling fictional universe, since for him, as for all good writers, the distinction between autobiography and fiction really matters only to the extent that one, at a particular moment, offers the imagination a greater latitude than the other. For with White we are in that border territory where memoir and fiction bleed into each other, as do eros and grief, humor and sorrow, banality and beauty.

Given White's frequent border crossings between fact and imagination, it's illuminating to see the full territory of his actual boyhood and adolescence laid out, the young life from which *A Boy's Own Story* was quarried. We learn in this biography, for instance, that when reading *The Catcher in the Rye* as a boy White couldn't understand Holden Caulfield's being so appalled by the world's phoniness. For the young Ed White it was self-evident that the world was very phony (as well as heartless, deluded, and selfish), and this deep-seated distrust of humanity throws interesting light on his subsequent aloofness from political concerns. To be an activist is to believe in the ultimate goodness and rationality of people, but White's alienated feeling of *me against them* persisted in him even as he came to know other gays.

We also learn that as a teenager in the repressive 1950s he was already shocking people with the casual sexual explicitness of his writing. Classmates (among them, Thomas McGuane) would snicker while White read out long descriptions of penises in Honors English class. Unaware of any literary precedent for openly gay writing (at the library it was not any book that clued him in on the existence of an on-going gay world but rather the graffiti he would raptly read in the library's men's room), the teenaged White can be seen as a political writer in the sense that sometimes the personal really *is* the political. At least it can be when the person is a young gay writer at a time when homosexuality was regarded as a crime and a mental illness and most gay people felt cowed into public silence.

One

Divided House

Like so many of Edmund White's reactions to the events of his extraordinary childhood and adolescence, his first reaction at age seven to his parents' decision to divorce is initially startling yet makes perfect sense once understood. His parents' divorce was for him "an accession into self-consciousness." Having overheard his parents conducting their "divorce conference" in which they discussed "their lives and our lives ('I cannot lead my life in this way,' 'The children have their whole lives before them')," young Eddie learned "that a life could be changed and that one could enter a brand-new, better world." More fundamentally, it was by learning that a life could be changed that the seven-year-old Eddie discovered he had a life at all—as well as an identity and a future.

This feeling that he hadn't quite started living until after his parents' divorce is symptomatic of how completely neglected he was as a small child. For the truth is that throughout his first seven years Ed was virtually ignored by his intimidating family and, for someone so sociable by nature (by puberty he would be equating existence itself with social interaction), such extreme isolation had a profound effect. This neglect, together with a sense of "anguish and conflict in the house," led little Eddie to become "very disassociated from other people. I was very withdrawn and self-loathing and rather uninterested in humanity in general."

Edmund White had the misfortune to be born into a family that, while small (there was just one sibling, his sister Margaret) and financially well-off, had no room for him emotionally and was beginning to fall apart. Margie, three and a half years older, was a strong-willed girl who resented her little brother's existence and rarely wanted anything to do with him. His father, called "E.V." (the initials of his first and middle names, Edmund Valentine), a rather terrifying and misanthropic man who'd never wanted children in the first place, had become more remote than ever from family life after having started up his own business about a year before Ed's birth. And his mother, Delilah, who later, after the divorce, would both burden and encourage her young son by becoming his "best friend," was at this point so consumed by the slowly crumbling state of her and E.V.'s marriage that she had little time for anything else.

E.V. and Delilah had both been born and raised in Texas, but they'd been living up north all their adult lives. E.V. was a physically strong man over six feet tall who in appearance—lanky, potbellied, long-faced, big-eared—somewhat resembled President Lyndon Johnson (a fellow Texan from the same age group). Delilah was quite tiny (just five feet tall), someone Ed would, as a teenager, laugh about with his sister because Delilah so much resembled Amanda Wingfield, the melodramatic, very southern mother in Tennessee Williams' *The Glass Menagerie* who speaks of "gentlemen callers" and is in the habit of waking her children up by calling out, "Rise and Shine!"

Delilah and E.V. had met at the College of Industrial Arts, a small women's junior college in Denton, Texas where Delilah was a student and E.V. the son of the school's dean. E.V. was just sixteen, two years younger than Delilah, when they started dating. Three years later, in 1924, the two got married on the spur of the moment, keeping the marriage a secret both because of E.V.'s youth (he gave his age as twenty-one on the marriage license but was in fact nineteen) and because E.V. rightly feared his parents' reaction to his marrying a girl clearly a cut below him socially. When E.V.'s parents did find out a short time later, his mother angrily confronted him by saying, "If you had to have sex, why didn't you go buy it?"

E.V.'s parents threatened at first to have the marriage annulled but then relented and let it stand. Later in life, after his twenty-three-year marriage to Delilah had ended in divorce, E.V. himself dismissed the marriage in the same terms his mother had flung in his face: it was a regrettable act of youthful folly committed out of an impatience to have sex.

After E.V. received a degree in Civil Engineering (with honors) from the University of Colorado, he and Delilah lived briefly in Gary, Indiana, where E.V. worked as an engineer for U.S. Steel, and then in Youngstown, Ohio. By late 1927 they'd moved to Cincinnati, where they would live out the final two decades of their marriage. Although E.V. and Delilah were both excessively talkative, upwardly mobile Texans who loved Cadillacs and symphonies and were glad to leave Texas behind for the opportunities of the north, the dramatic differences between them were all too apparent. For along with their huge difference in height, they were also polar opposites in temperament and beliefs. He was stoic and cold, while she was warm and impulsive; she had a very personal connection to God, often talking to him "one-on-one," while he declared that he would never set foot "in any god-damned church." He was conservative and frankly racist, while she was liberal and, decades before it became a matter of course for educated white Americans, proud of her enlightened attitude towards black people. He was a misanthrope who preferred things to people and who later in life avoided his own employees by working at night, while she had a tireless interest in and curiosity about people. And while Delilah could be a reckless spendthrift inclined to live beyond her means, E.V., for all the money he accumulated, was always stringent and dully responsible in financial matters. Finally, while E.V.'s travels never took him outside North America, Delilah spent the second half of her long life happily globe-trotting. It was because his parents were such a pair of opposites that Eddie felt, long before their divorce, that he lived in a "divided house."

The steady unravelling of E.V. and Delilah's marriage and Ed's birth in 1940 came to seem so interrelated that one day in 1947, soon after the divorce, seven-year-old Eddie broke down and began sobbing uncontrollably. Delilah had taken to implying none too subtly to her young son that his being born had set in motion the events that led to the divorce and Eddie, who personally welcomed the divorce as a "deliverance" from his frightening father, had burst into tears because he felt responsible for his mother's anguish. This terrible anguish of his mother's went a long way towards forming the dark side of Edmund White's underlying character. Years before his troubled feelings about homosexuality would accentuate all this in him still further, the unhappiness that filled his mother from practically the time he was born created in Ed an enormous, free-floating sense of guilt as well as a fundamental insecurity about his place with people that has led him throughout his life to put an unusual amount of effort into pleasing and winning over everyone around him.

Because Delilah's anguish had such a devastating effect on both her and Ed, it's worth looking into what actually broke up her marriage to E.V. Their divorce can be seen now as the consequence not so much of Ed's birth as of Delilah's inability to tend simultaneously to two "babies": her infant son and her husband. In 1939 E.V. had decided to found his own company, the White Industrial Sales & Equipment Company, because he'd grown fed up with the Cincinnati chemical company he'd worked for as a salesman for the past several years after they'd failed to extend the promotion he'd both expected and believed he deserved. Ironically, it was Delilah who provided her cautious husband with the final push of encouragement he needed to take the plunge and go into business for himself—ironic, because E.V.'s new business set up a situation in which Delilah would be found unworthy as a wife.

By 1941, when Eddie was a one-year-old toddler, E.V. was struggling to make White Industrial Sales a success and had adopted the nocturnal schedule—rising late in the afternoon and working throughout the night—that was most natural to him and that he would adhere to for the rest of his life. He began to insist that Delilah accompany him to the office each night because he wanted her by his side as he worked. But after several weeks of this Delilah begged off, complaining that sitting up all night with him had so exhausted her that it was threatening her health. It was at this point that E.V. began to turn more and more to his secretary, Kay Beard, who was soon giving him everything he needed from a woman and helpmate. Kay was the third employee E.V. had hired, and the first from outside the family (his younger brother Bill White and wife Helen were on the staff from the beginning). After several years as his mistress, Kay became—just weeks after E.V.'s divorce from Delilah had gone through—his second wife. Kay's union with E.V. now looks so natural and inevitable, particularly given how poorly matched E.V. and Delilah were, that the only surprise, really, is that they waited six long years before tying the knot. This delay had nothing to do with the quality of their rapport and everything to do with E.V.'s hesitancy to risk scaring off business in conservative Cincinnati by tainting his image with a scandalous divorce.

What won E.V.'s heart was clearly the intense, single-minded, around-the-clock devotion to him that Kay displayed, a devotion that compared so favorably with Delilah's self-centered grumbling. During these last years of marriage to Delilah, E.V.'s life revolved solely around White Industrial Sales. He spent nearly every waking hour at the office, engrossed in the risky enterprise of making and keeping his company financially viable, and even if he hadn't been conducting a love affair with Kay he still would have seen infinitely more of her than he did Delilah back at home. When he was with Delilah, what he saw all too often was a spendthrift wife who had the annoying habit, moreover, of praying aloud each time they were about to have sex.

Then too, when Delilah went back to school to study psychology in 1943 she took to psychoanalyzing him, something he found both fatuous and irritating. Kay, by contrast, was not only devoted to him but genuinely interested in his business (which was virtually his only interest), throwing herself into managing the books and typing his correspondence. And though Kay was a farm girl from Carey, Ohio with a high school education, she was nonetheless much better at sweet-talking clients at business luncheons than Delilah, who had an egotistical and charmless way of leading nearly every conversation, no matter the topic, back to flattering stories about herself. E.V. may have even had the example of his own father in mind. "Dean White," as E.V.'s father was known, was repeatedly forced to turn down the presidency of his junior college because he felt his eccentric wife, Ollie Martin White—a strong-willed, loose cannon of a woman who refused to cook, among other things, declaring it to be a waste of time and thus forcing them to take their meals at the college cafeteria or at a nearby boarding house all their married lives—would only embarrass him amidst all the entertaining a college president must do.

E.V.'s sister-in-law Helen White knew both Kay and Delilah at this time, since she both worked alongside Kay at the office and lived for a time with E.V. and Delilah. Helen observed that E.V. seemed to prefer Kay to Delilah because he himself was quite competitive and he disliked Delilah's strong personality, which had a way of "attracting all the attention." Delilah's tragedy was that desperate as she was to hold on to E.V., she was at the same time constitutionally incapable of taking a backseat to a man who needed precisely that. Kay, on the other hand, was far more conventional in that her ambitions were limited to her status in Cincinnati's social world and thus dovetailed neatly and traditionally with E.V.'s business aspirations.

That Edmund White was born at all was a lucky quirk of fate. Delilah had had to plead with E.V. at length each time she wanted to have a child before winning his reluctant consent (in not wanting children, E.V., oddly enough, was taking after his own mother, who had made a point of telling E.V. as a boy that she'd daily tried to abort him by beating her stomach with her fists while pregnant with him). In 1934 Delilah had given birth to a first child, Carolyn, who'd died of a cerebral hemorrhage after only a few hours. Had Carolyn lived, E.V. almost certainly would have drawn the line at two children following the birth of their second daughter, Margie.

As a woman who waited until her thirties to have children, Delilah had complications with all three of her births. Following Margie's birth there had been a brief scare during which it seemed possible that she too might die. And shortly after Eddie was born he suffered a convulsion or seizure while he and Delilah were still in the hospital. Because she was now thirty-six, Delilah was advised by her doctor not to have any more children and to name Eddie "caboose." The infant Eddie quickly recovered and the mysterious seizure was soon forgotten. What Delilah did remember—and never tired of proclaiming throughout the rest of her life—was that Eddie's special nature had been immediately apparent: he "had the largest head I had ever seen on a newborn. The large head and small body made him look like a tadpole."

E.V. may have never wanted children but Eddie was nonetheless his only son and Eddie's birth on January 13, 1940 filled E.V. with an "abstract, dynastic" pride; in a rare burst of personal effusiveness, he telephoned everyone he knew to say he had a son. This dynastic pride was also reflected in Eddie's being named Edmund Valentine White III. In everyday life, however, E.V. was soon disappointed by how meek and unathletic his little son was turning out to be; in the end, E.V. showed even less interest in Eddie than he did in Margie. It didn't help matters that Eddie could also be an effeminate little boy, fascinated by "women's stuff" such as nail polish and perfume and occasionally prone to walking about wearing Delilah's hats and carrying her purse.

The scant amount of attention Delilah paid her children was unusual even in the upper-middle-class Cincinnati world of the 1940s that E.V. and Delilah inhabited, a world where live-in black "help" allowed wives—as housewives relieved of housework and child care—to attend Friday matinee concerts of the Cincinnati Symphony Orchestra. But though neither E.V. nor Delilah, as deeply preoccupied parents, took much of an active interest in the children, it came to be understood that Margie was E.V.'s child while Eddie was Delilah's. And interestingly, in a family in which both children would grow up to be gay, it was Margie who became, by default, E.V.'s "true son" in that it was she who was the athlete, who showed competitive fire, and who would play rousing Ping-Pong games with her father. An unexpected, embarrassing spotlight was trained on Eddie's and Margie's gender-bending one summer when an outspoken lifeguard, having watched the two of them at play on the beach, shouted down to Margie, "You should have been the boy and he should have been the girl!"

Eddie, who had inherited his mother's warm brown eyes and sociable disposition, came to think of his father and sister, with their fair hair and hard-driving personalities, as "the Aryans" of the family. Early photos and home movies of Margie and Eddie point up the differences between them: Margie "a tall, taut platinum blonde," confident and icy-eyed, and Eddie a sweet and somewhat frail little boy in a sailor suit. But though Delilah had taken to exhibiting her own baby photo side by side with a baby photo of Eddie, proudly declaring that "Everyone who visits says, 'Oh Delilah, you two look so much alike with your big brown eyes!'," Eddie had in fact inherited many more of his father's features, from E.V.'s long face and high forehead to his big jug ears, deep-set eyes, and thin-lipped, wobbly mouth.

Yet Eddie was so far from being his father's son that fear would always be uppermost in his feelings for E.V., even long after Ed had become an adult. Two vivid scenes in Ed's autobiographical novel *A Boy's Own Story* define his relationship to his father in the years before the divorce. In the first scene the Boy (as I will call the unnamed narrator of *A Boy's Own Story*), who rarely sees his mysterious father because of the father's eccentric nocturnal schedule, is prodded by his mother late one afternoon into entering the bedroom of his just-awakened father and giving him a back rub: "On the bed, face down, lay my naked father under sheets, like a sea monster beached and sick in a tide pool of foam. The mingled smells of night sweat and stale cigar smoke awed me...."

Now that the father's mysterious and intimidating presence has been established, the decisive encounter between father and son is presented. The Boy has been bad and his mother has asked the father to punish the Boy by whipping him with a leather belt. After the father marches his son into the master bedroom and orders him to drop his pants, the Boy finds he

> *... had already started a sort of gasping, an asthmatic gasping, in anticipation of a pain that seemed impossibly cruel because I had no idea when it would descend on me nor how long it would last. My lack of control over the situation was for me the worst pun-*

ishment, and I gasped and gasped for air and escape and justice, or at least mercy....

But he was angry now. His hate, more intense than any other feeling he'd ever had for me, was making his face younger and younger. His eyes no longer had that veiled, compounded look of adults.... Now his eyes were simple and curious, eyes I recognized as those of another child. A scream caught up with me and outraced me.... It took me over and wouldn't stop. It was a cry of outrage against a violation at the hands of a child no older than I but much less appeasable—a heartless boy.

He tugged my pants down and pushed me forward into the glossy spread. The belt fell again and again, much too long and much too harshly to my mind, which had suddenly turned strangely epicurean. The solace of the condemned is scorn, especially scorn of an aesthetic stripe. In that moment the vital energies retreated out of my body into a small, hard gland of bitter objectivity, a gland that would secrete its poison through me for the rest of my life.

Unmentioned in the novel (but adding to the terror, the torture of the experience) is that, hours before E.V. arrived on the scene, Delilah had already told Eddie that he was going to be beaten—something that condemned him to a "long period of suspense" while waiting for his father to come home and administer the punishment. But what is even more striking than the Boy's terror in this passage is the perception that the father had suddenly become an enormous child himself, "a heartless boy" whose sadistic relish inflicts upon the Boy's mind a lasting and poisoned sense of "bitter objectivity." "It's one thing if your father loves you and it hurts him as much as it hurts you," Ed says of the belt whipping, explaining that because E.V. had instead made him feel he was "in the hands of a tyrant" the effect was to create in him a "deep distrust, a feeling of alienation" towards his parents and, by extension, towards the world at large. For by "bitter objectivity" Ed meant a loss of faith in people, a feeling of "me against them" that he would continue to feel even as a gay adult among gay people. This loss of faith made Eddie realize—at the tender age of three—that "currying favor" and "dissembling" were the best means of dealing with people (a habit of mind that became so ingrained in him that by the time he read *The Catcher in the Rye* as a teenager, for example, Holden Caulfield's being "so appalled by the world's phoniness never made sense to me because I'd never thought the world was anything but phony").

The belt whipping was also Eddie's introduction to betrayal, and because it had been his mother's idea in the first place that he be whipped, Eddie viewed the whole experience as a "double betrayal." This sense of having been cruelly betrayed is the origin of another habit of mind Ed has kept for a lifetime: "When I'm betrayed, I'm never surprised." In the life of someone who would go on to betray others himself—for, as will be seen, Ed's betrayals were to become an important theme with many variations— Delilah and E.V.'s betrayal of their little son can be seen as a kind of original sin. (Of course, it could also be argued that it was rather Eddie's extreme reaction to being whipped that led to all these fundamental attitudes and habits of mind in him. E.V., for instance, had been whipped as a boy with a birch branch by his father—whippings that E.V. would later credit with having "knocked some sense" into him.)

If Eddie feared his father, he also feared his older sister Margie (indeed, in *A Boy's Own Story* the sister also wields a sadistic belt). Moreover, just as E.V. was intimidating yet largely unavailable, so too was Margie someone who both held herself aloof from Eddie and occasionally tormented him. In fact, what usually provoked Margie's ire was precisely Eddie's attempts to join her and her circle of friends from Miss Doherty's School for Girls in play.

> *My sister resented the interest some of the girls took in me and banned me from the meetings held beside the empty swimming pool choked with dead leaves. When I disobeyed her and toddled smilingly into the assembly, she spanked my bare legs with a hairbrush. My father, resolved that his son should hold his own, pinioned my sister's arms behind her and ordered me to switch her on the back*

of her legs with a stinging branch. But I knew that soon enough he would disappear again, my mother drive off, the maids look away; I dropped the branch, howled and clattered up the stairs to my room.

The belt whipping, the confrontations by the empty swimming pool, and all the other events of Ed's early childhood took place in and around the White family house at 8 Beech Lane in Cincinnati's East Walnut Hills. The house stood at the end of a shady lane and overlooked a steep, wooded ravine. These woods gave the property a remote feel (as did the gloomy and mysterious Home for the Incurables which stood nearby) and it was easy to forget that Madison Road, a four-lane thoroughfare thronging with cars and trolleys, lay just two blocks away. It was also hard to imagine that Beech Lane, just two blocks long, was in fact an enclave situated in a kind of border zone between the far wealthier homes to the east and the much poorer, and largely black, quarter to the west. This in-between position was mirrored in the family's financial standing. For the Whites were now "at the lower end of the upper crust" (the Beech Lane house, which they rented for one hundred dollars a month, while nice enough was nonetheless much smaller than the houses of Margie's classmates at Miss Doherty's; the father of one friend, for instance, was a vice president at Proctor and Gamble).

Margie was sometimes capable of inflicting "really mean things" on her little brother for no reason at all. The middle finger of Ed's right hand, for example, is still slightly indented near its tip from the time Margie asked him to place it in the hinge of an escritoire she had in her room: when her trusting little brother dutifully did as he was told, Margie promptly closed the hinge on the finger. And yet at other times Margie—to her own surprise—could be her brother's protector. Once, when Eddie was three, he'd had a nasty run-in with a neighborhood bully named Rodney while riding his tricycle down Beech Lane. When Margie learned what Rodney had done, she "just about killed this kid," telling him, "You leave my little brother alone!" Afterwards, Margie felt "shocked that I was that protective."

Margie and Eddie got along much better during the long

vacations the family would spend each summer on Mullet Lake in northern Michigan, possibly because at Mullet Lake Margie was without her "tribe of girls"—her circle of friends from Miss Doherty's. The family had originally started coming to northern Michigan as a means of providing Margie some relief from her allergies (Mullet Lake being far enough north to be above the "pollen line"), and after staying in rented cottages the first few summers, E.V. eventually bought a seven-bedroom summer house on the lake that was bigger than the Beech Lane house in Cincinnati. In this enormous summer "cottage" Eddie and Margie spent hours entertaining themselves by "dressing up and doing all these 'shows'" in a separate apartment above the garage.

It was while up at Mullet Lake one summer that Delilah was confronted with some shocking news that made it impossible for her to continue to overlook what was going on between her husband and his secretary, Kay Beard. As had become the family's established routine, Delilah and the two children (along with Anna, the live-in black help) had gone to Mullet Lake for the summer while E.V. remained at work in Cincinnati, visiting them when he could on weekends. Accompanying them this particular summer was E.V.'s mother, known by Delilah as "Mother White." Mother White had long forgotten her old wish to have E.V. and Delilah's marriage annulled and over the years had become friends with Delilah, even managing to talk Delilah into converting to Christian Science for a time.

Colorful Mother White was a stylish, formal-looking woman with delicate, porcelain skin and carefully kept hair who nonetheless loved to gamble on horse races as well as perform rough chores such as replacing shingles on the roof. By way of explanation for her "dual personality," she would say, "I was born with an inner war. My mother was a beautiful, refined woman from Ohio, while my father was a cotton-buying, horse-trading rough man from Texas." In addition to refusing to cook for her husband, Mother White also declined to keep house or sleep with him. She could also be quite domineering, never hesitating to meddle in the lives of those around her. Unasked, she would set about rearranging the furniture in the home of her other daughter-in-law, Helen White, for example, and had once dragged Helen into a department store they happened to be passing because she didn't like the hat Helen had on. Then too, she had tried but failed to spirit her prettiest granddaughter, Sue White, off to Hollywood where she was convinced Sue could become the new Shirley Temple.

Soon after arriving at Mullet Lake this particular summer, Mother White dropped a bombshell on Delilah: "You are losing your husband to another woman, and I am returning to Cincinnati, by bus, to look into the whole matter." Sure enough, Mother White discovered upon her return that E.V. had moved Kay Beard into 8 Beech Lane. In the ensuing showdown over E.V.'s adultery, E.V. ended up ordering Mother White to leave the house and never come back. It turned out to be a decisive encounter between him and his mother for, as it happened, Mother White never did return to Cincinnati (she died just a few years later).

Even taking into account how truly scandalous adultery and divorce were in the middle America of the 1940s, it's striking that E.V. and his mother never patched up their rift. After all, E.V. had always been crazy about his mother, who like him was a night owl; when the two of them were visiting with each other they would sit up and talk all night. As a boy E.V. had faithfully served her, daily brushing out her beautiful hair and doing the laborious work—in those days before washing machines—of washing the family laundry by hand. What is more surprising is that E.V. also admired his difficult, nutty mother more than he did his father, dean of a women's college for thirty years, because his mother had gumption, energy, and an independent streak (in a small, informal way she was also a shrewd businesswoman) whereas his father, who "did everything by the clock," merely subsisted on a college salary. Yet Mother White's favorite son had always been not E.V. but her much less ambitious younger son Bill, whom she had sometimes kept home from school so that he could do the housework she loathed and keep her company.

When Mother White died there was talk of a "family melancholia" and rumors that she had committed suicide. Moreover, on the day she died Eddie happened to peek into his father's study and "found him standing behind my sister's chair, brushing her hair and crying."

Now that Delilah had been jolted by evidence of how serious her husband's affair with Kay had become, she reacted by making plans to attend graduate school—enrolling that fall in a master's degree program in psychology at the University of Cincinnati. Delilah had always nursed ambitions of her own. As a teenager she'd struggled with her mother and stepfather to be allowed to go to college at all and several years into her marriage, in 1934, she'd gone back to complete the undergraduate studies she'd left unfinished when she married E.V. At that time her return to school had been motivated by a competitive urge to stay abreast of her husband's growing professional success in some way.

Now in the fall of 1943 she was motivated by what was quite clearly panic about the uncertainties suddenly on the horizon. But though her instinct about preparing herself for a possible life as a divorcée proved accurate, the divorce was still more than three long years in the future. In the meantime salvaging the marriage still seemed possible, if she could just ride out the storm. And yet what is so clear now is that by holding out such hopes she only lay herself open to new heights of torment. For the latter months of 1943 marked the beginning of what would be several years of anguish for Delilah as she struggled to live with E.V. and Kay's affair much as someone slowly going mad might watch her mental state deteriorating with a mixture of helplessness and shame (she never told her parents what was happening until the very end of the marriage).

As it happened, Delilah's return to school was linked with the beginning of Eddie's education, for they both entered programs at the University of Cincinnati. Three-year-old Eddie began attending the University's demonstration nursery school. As Delilah's self-published autobiography, *Delilah: A Life in Progress*, would have it, the idea of pursuing a master's degree happened to occur to her as a means of productively passing the time while waiting to drive her son back from nursery school each day (gas rationing during these war years limiting her to only one trip to the University per day). Yet because this fall was also the beginning of her mounting alarm about E.V. and Kay, it seems far more likely that it was the other way around—Delilah opted to go to the University herself and then found it convenient to enroll Eddie there as well. This likely rearrangement of the truth is a revealing example of Delilah's habit of portraying herself (both to herself and to others) as having been far more selfless and devoted to her children than was actually the case.

The demonstration nursery school was overseen by a Dr. Arlitt, a specialist in child psychology who also happened to be Delilah's teacher and mentor in the psychology department at the University of Cincinnati and whose theories on child psychology Delilah would continue to quote to Eddie and Margie for years to come. Yet (somewhat mysteriously) after attending the demonstration nursery school for a year, Eddie was not invited back for a second year at the school (even though, at age four, he was still a year shy of starting kindergarten). Part of the mystery of Eddie's "dismissal" lies in his having been, at least in some respects, a model student. As Delilah saw it:

> [Eddie] *has a quality that is extremely rare in the young child and he seems to have had it from the beginning and that is a sympathetic understanding for the problems and sufferings of others. Dr. Arlitt pointed out these qualities in his nursery school days as being almost never heard of in the three year old. The average young child is by nature a little animal, grasping and selfish.*

Ed's own recollections confirm this: "I was considered very unusual as a child because I was very altruistic. Apparently I was not only concerned about the other children but also about the teachers. I would say things like, 'You look very tired today. Do you take a nap?' And that was considered astounding and weird."

When Dr. Arlitt told Delilah that Eddie would not be invited back for a second year, all that Arlitt offered by way of explanation was that in his need to continually "administer" to the other children Eddie "wasn't one of them"—that is, didn't fit in with his classmates—and that for a young boy to display such an acute sense of responsibility must mean that the situation was putting him under too great a strain. (Overhearing Ed discussing, in 1996, his year at nursery school, his lover, Michael Carroll, said to him: "You mean, you were running around making sure everyone was all right even then? You're still doing that today.") While Dr. Arlitt was probably putting the best possible face on the situation (after all, Delilah was Arlitt's student in the psychology department), this notion of Eddie's having been a little boy who in his constant fussing over everyone wasn't one of the gang likely contains the essence of the real explanation. For the reasons for Eddie's dismissal almost certainly involved his being a disruption to the natural order of the classroom. Dr. Arlitt, who had set up the demonstration nursery school as a kind of laboratory in which to study young children's behavior in general, would not have been interested in any individual child, especially one so unusual as Eddie. Then too, Eddie was "undersocialized" and "probably didn't know how to play with other kids," and thus was probably perceived by the nursery school staff as being "too neurotic" and "overwrought" and more trouble than he was worth.

What is fascinating about this early glimpse into Eddie's behavior is how many fundamental elements of his personality, along with some major themes of his boyhood, were already in place. For if Delilah and Dr. Arlitt had found Eddie's precocious compassion for others astounding, they would have been even more astonished had they known that this compassion was something that Eddie was consciously affecting. Each time he was praised by the nursery school staff, young Eddie would feel guilty because he knew he had won the praise through deviousness.

At the remarkably early age of three Eddie had come to feel that it was not enough to act "naturally"; people had to be courted—an outlook that originated partly in his having discovered that his distracted mother "responded so well when you babied her." Of course, Eddie's courting of people also had its roots in the "double betrayal" of the belt whipping and his consequent loss of faith in people. But the very idea of a three-year-old boy's having to "baby" his mother suggests that the erratic and provisional nature of Delilah's love and attention gave Eddie such an enfeebled sense of his own self-worth that he'd concluded that people would not take an interest in him unless he courted them. Moreover, these early feelings of insecurity would seem to be the origin of what some people have seen as the "almost crazy" need Ed has had nearly all his life to win the affection of hundreds, if not thousands of people (people such as Ed's former editor Michael Denneny, for example, have been bewildered by his seemingly bottomless appetite for meeting and winning over new people). Finally, Eddie's having been a three-year-old who felt forced to pretend he cared about and sympathized with his mother's problems may help to explain the sometimes ambiguous nature of his kindness—an ambiguity that people who know Ed today can't help but sense lies behind the artful solicitousness of his personal charm.

Doubting himself and his instincts, acting deviously, and feeling guilty about his deviousness were feelings and habits of mind that would stay with Ed all through his youth and into adulthood. His experience at the demonstration nursery school also introduced him to what would become two more themes of his youth: his involvement in the world of psychological evaluation, and his being an adult-oriented boy who was not completely at ease with other children. It's ironic, if not entirely unusual, that Delilah was studying child psychology at the very time she was helping to make her own child so neurotic that he was unable to integrate himself properly into his first real encounter with children his own age (after all, Delilah had enrolled Eddie in nursery school specifically because she felt "he needed children his own age with whom to play"). But what was truly odd was that Delilah had become "so totally self-absorbed" that she never even considered enrolling Eddie in a new nursery school the following year, a decision that left him to languish at home by himself throughout the 1944/45 school year. It was to be the loneliest time in his life.

During this lonely year Eddie spent at home alone as a four- and five-year-old, he cried every morning as Margie and Delilah left the house. Eddie was not technically alone, however, for Anna, the live-in help Delilah had engaged after Eddie's birth who stayed with the family until the divorce, was on hand.* Anna was someone Eddie had seen far more of than his own mother—when he was an infant it was Anna who slept each night beside his crib. Even when Eddie was two and three, Anna would often sleep on a cot in his bedroom, allowing him to sleep in her "governing shade and disturbingly intimate smell." In part because he was afraid of the dark, Eddie had become so attached to having Anna sleeping beside him that E.V. declared, in one of his more awful and memorable statements, that "That boy can't go to sleep without the smell of nigger in his nostrils."

The demeaning racism prevalent in the white Cincinnati of the 1940s is also reflected in Anna's having been privately referred to at times within the family as "Black Anna." For her part, the true nature of Anna's feelings for the family likely had much to do with being a black woman trapped in an overtly racist world where she was exploited as cheap labor by whites—by the Whites, in her case. Far from having been a second or true mother to Eddie, Anna was actually a "cold fish" who never talked or played with him and merely endured his presence. "She had the housework to do, of course; she wasn't a nanny, she was a maid, really. She was always sweeping and looking kind of gruff and saying, 'Get in here and eat your lunch.' I don't think there was any love wasted. I think Mother probably hired her thinking she'd be this nice warm black woman who would be this sort of Aunt Jemima type."

But if Delilah found it convenient to sentimentalize Anna and her relationship with Eddie, Ed's psychiatrist in the 1970s, Dr. Charles Silverstein (with whom Ed would cowrite *The Joy of Gay Sex*), tried to make Anna into a sexual abuser. "I remember Dr. Silverstein used to speculate that there had been some sexual abuse of me by her. He thought my fear of her was way out of line

* Although Anna does not figure in *A Boy's Own Story*, she is a minor character in Ed's earlier novel *Nocturnes for the King of Naples* (1978), where we learn of the "tiny attic room" she slept in, "its ceiling sloped and smelling of copper and electricity." In *Boy's Own* there are only two fleeting and indirect references to being left in the care of a "nurse." Anna is also referred to as a nurse in *Nocturnes*. In real life, however, she was not a nurse but a domestic who cooked and kept house.

and must be explained by some other problem." But this never rang true for Ed; his own explanation for his fear of Anna is simply that he was responding to the considerable "anger and pride in Anna. I feel like I've always been very sensitive to black anger against white people and I think it shows up in *Blue Boy in Black*— a play Ed would write in college about a black maid and gardener who set out to destroy the white family they work for.

Nevertheless, it was Eddie's unwitting racial insensitivity that led him to thoughtlessly insult Anna once—something that constituted another great trauma of his early childhood. "There was a rhyme that I'd learned from the other kids, maybe my sister: 'Eenie meenie mainnie moe, catch a nigger by the toe....' I was sitting idly saying that to myself in an armchair in the living room, and the maid heard me and she was furious. I felt so bad—I hadn't even thought what the words meant." When Anna, deeply offended, reproached him, Eddie "went racing up to the attic and hid myself there. My mother finally came home and found me up in the attic and said, 'Well, you have to go down and apologize.' To me, that was one of the most terrifying things I'd ever done."

It was during this lonely year at home that Eddie invented three imaginary playmates: Cottage Cheese, Georgie-Porgie, and Tom-Thumb-Thumb (which the four-year-old Eddie pronounced "Tom-Shum-Shum").

Cottage Cheese, the girl, was older than I, sensible and bossy but my ally. She and I tolerated our good-natured younger sidekick, Georgie-Porgie, a dimwit we fussed over for his own good. We felt nothing of this benign condescension toward Tom-Thumb-Thumb, the hellion who roamed the woods beyond the barbed wire guarding the neighbor's property, off limits to us and to him too, I'm sure, though he ignored this rule and all others. He was just a rustle of dried leaves, a panting of quick hot breath behind the honeysuckle, a blur of tanned leg and muddy knees or a distant hoot and holler—an irrepressible male freedom (all the freer because he was a boy and not a man). He needed no one....

[Tom-Thumb-Thumb] *never cared for me. Cottage Cheese and I, determined that naive Georgie-Porgie should not fall under Tom's spell, made a great show of listing Tom's faults—but privately I worried about Tom and at night I wondered where he was sleeping, was he dry, was he warm, hungry. I even envied his sovereignty, though the price of freedom—total solitude—seemed more than I could possibly pay.*

Tom's independence and Georgie's dependence rendered them both unsatisfactory as playmates. If the family was going on a trip I gladly left the boys behind so long as I could take Cottage Cheese with me.

Ed today finds it interesting that there's only one girl but two boys—as though he needed two characters to express his feelings about being a boy and about boys in general. Moreover, that both invented boys were not, in practice, playmates at all (since Tom didn't want to play with Eddie—or anyone—and Eddie didn't want to play with Georgie) strikes Ed as a perfect illustration of Freud's concept of the repetition compulsion, as laid out in *Beyond the Pleasure Principle*, which holds that children in play will re-create painful experiences in order to gain mastery over their fears.

Georgie-Porgie can be seen as a kid brother who allowed Eddie to play an older sibling who treated his kid brother not with the cruel contempt of Eddie's real sister, Margie, but with a tolerance that, while condescending, included real concern. Tom-Thumb-Thumb, on the other hand, was almost certainly inspired by the "bad boys" who played down in the thickly wooded ravine behind the White home on Beech Lane. Eddie himself often spent whole days exploring the two acres of woods at the bottom of the ravine, following the little stream that flowed from an open sewer, accompanied by the family dog, Timmy. At night these older boys, whom Eddie envied and feared and found fascinating, could be heard "hollooing to one another" down in the darkness. "There was this menacing feeling that the waifs of the city were going through this otherwise idyllic wood." Eddie's fascination with Tom-Thumb-Thumb and the bad boys was the beginning of a lifelong fascination with wild boys—a theme that would go on to encompass everything from the first boy Ed had sex with (a kind of retarded wild boy) to explaining some of his attraction, as an adult, to the life of Jean Genet.

Cottage Cheese seems a clear example of simple wish fulfillment: she's the older sister he wished he'd had, as bossy as he'd seen his real sister being with her friends but otherwise appealingly different—a friendly companion as well as an ally and advisor.

Most important of all, these imaginary playmates constitute an early example of the theme of "the exaggerated consolations of the imagination" in Ed's youth. Eddie initially had been drawn into the world of the imagination when—on his third birthday, during a performance of *Sleeping Beauty* given at the Beech Lane house by a marionette troupe—he found the puppet characters easier to understand and thus more real than the "opaque" people around him in real life. When Eddie turned to inventing characters of his own (his imaginary playmates), however, he discovered two unexpectedly unpleasant aspects of the imagination: that its creations are more real to the observer than to the creator, and that the act of creative imagination is itself an "admission of some sort of failure."

Eddie had first realized that creations are more real to the observer than the creator by noticing that the puppets in the performance of *Sleeping Beauty*, while "stronger than life" to him, the observer, were "feeble" creations to the puppeteers themselves; conversely, while he himself "didn't really like my imaginary friends precisely because they were so irritatingly vague and unreal," these creatures were "almost, at times, less real to me than to my indulgent mother...." As for creative imagination being an admission of failure, this truth was self-evident from the time he invented Cottage Cheese, Georgie, and Tom; after all, he'd been forced to resort to these unsatisfying playmates in the first place only because no real children, such as his sister, would play with him. The theme of the exaggerated consolations of the imagination can thus be more precisely defined as the disappointing level of reality offered by *one's own* imaginative creations (for as Ed would discover as an adult author, it was only books written by others that he could find satisfying).

Not surprisingly, learning to read was something Eddie experienced as a dramatic breakthrough, for books provided easy access to the more convincing creations of other people. Reading liberated him from himself and his immediate surroundings. Ed would later compare the experience to a door swinging open in a stuffy room, because soon after learning to read he happened to walk into his mother's bathroom one day and as the two of them talked while she lay in the bath it suddenly dawned on him that, in books, he had discovered that he now possessed "this incredible escape hatch any time I wanted it" and could thus be "free of her and everybody else." By having learned to read he was no longer completely dependent on the whims of his often indifferent family and no longer limited to the world of his own creative imagination.

Anyone who knows the brilliantly fluent speaker Edmund White has been throughout his adult life might be surprised to learn that he had a rather serious stuttering problem as a little boy. One possible cause for this stuttering may have been Eddie's odd isolation and lack of real—that is, human—playmates. There may also have been a genetic component; Delilah's brother, Jack Teddlie, had stuttered so terribly as a child that, like Demosthenes, he took to stuffing pebbles in his mouth. Then too, by the time he was three or four Eddie had become very high strung (as he would remain all through his youth and into early adulthood). Whatever the cause of his stuttering, when Eddie was about five Delilah grew concerned enough about the problem to send him to a psychologist whose treatment centered around getting him to relax. "I would go to this woman often and I would lie down and she would sit beside me and lift my arms and let them drop. Then lift my feet up and down. And lift my head and let it gently fall back. It must have been hypnosis because she kept saying, 'You're a rag doll, you're a rag doll.' And then: 'You're falling, falling. Your body's very heavy, it's going through the bed. You're falling through the clouds,' and so on."

In this deeply relaxed state, Eddie was eventually able, when prompted by the psychologist, to speak whole sentences without stuttering. The psychologist's eventual diagnosis was that his stuttering had been caused by the family's habit of consistently silencing him. Nearly every night at the dinner table, for instance,

Eddie would throw a temper tantrum and knock over his glass of milk after being told to be quiet. For all this, given what we know of Eddie's fear of his father, the ultimate cure for his stuttering may simply have been getting away, after the divorce, from E.V.

Despite the growing tensions underlying their marriage, E.V. and Delilah still threw occasional cocktail parties. It was their habit, once the liquor and good cheer had started flowing, to rouse their children from their beds and have them come down to perform for guests in the large living room overlooking the woods. Eddie, who could be "very affable and social" in the company of adults even as a small boy, would play the piano in an untrained, tinkling sort of way, improvising on a theme that he'd worked out and named "The Brook." This composition, which can be seen as Ed's first artistic creation, took its name from the brook that ran behind the summer house at Mullet Lake. Margie and Eddie both "had this tremendous fascination with the brook," and after Eddie had created "The Brook" he would improvise on it both alone and in four-handed versions with Margie. But while Margie remembers it as "sounding pretty good," Ed himself believes that "it was probably just god-awful noise but Mother thought it was brilliant." In any event, over the next few years Eddie (who'd started taking proper lessons) occasionally indulged himself in fantasies of becoming a concert pianist until one fateful evening, a few years after the divorce, when he gave a performance of "The Brook" to some of Delilah's friends and they "just put their hands over their ears and screamed: 'Stop it, it's horrible!'" Eddie realized at that moment that "I was no longer a child prodigy of three but a boy of eight who was just annoying everybody. And I remember that was a big shock for me because I thought it actually was brilliant." Although he now had been shamed into giving up public performances on the piano, Eddie nonetheless continued to take lessons, "but only because I was forced to by my mother. I never liked it, and I was never good at it, and I never practiced."

Margie, for her part, would entertain her parents' guests by curtsying and singing songs in French—the courtesan skills she'd acquired at Miss Doherty's School for Girls. Showing off their children seems to have been both a very Texan practice on Delilah and E.V.'s part (Texas being a place where people will announce at a gathering: "Now Mary Jane is really good in spelling. Now come out here and spell...."), as well as a reflection of their both being so "narcissistic" that providing their guests with an amusing diversion took precedence over their children's sleep.

It was probably not entirely coincidental that once Delilah had received her master's degree in June of 1946 (her thesis was "The Development of Religious Concepts in the Young Child"), E.V. and Delilah's marriage became even more strained. For it seems probable that—now that Delilah was armed with a means of making her way in the world—Kay began to press E.V. more urgently to leave Delilah. In any event, there is a sense of the affair with Kay inexorably deepening over what turned out to be the last year of E.V. and Delilah's marriage. After years of discreet adultery with Kay, E.V. suddenly became careless enough to allow Delilah to find lipstick on the collar of one of his shirts.

Angered by having such classic, trite evidence thrown in her face, Delilah "drove to the office and blew the horn of my car (we had a special horn signal). When he came down to the street, I screamed at him accusingly and held the shirt up for him to see. He never said a word but went back to the office." By New Year's Eve things were coming to a head. Delilah and E.V. were invited to a party and, after initially refusing to attend it, E.V. reluctantly agreed to go on the condition that he be allowed to work at his office first before returning home to escort Delilah to the party later in the evening. Yet as the hour grew later and later there was no sign of him and, strangely, no answer when Delilah telephoned his office. At last Delilah drove to the office. "The doorman at the building announced me; as I entered the office there seemed to be an unusual tension. I was to learn later that [Kay] was with him and had hidden herself in the closet."

A few days later (early January being a time of new resolutions), Kay forced a showdown with Delilah. E.V. and Delilah had tickets to the Cincinnati Symphony Orchestra's Saturday night series and on the evening of January 4, 1947 Kay actually appeared at the concert hall and sat herself directly behind Delilah and E.V. Afterwards, E.V. took both women out for a tense meal before dropping Kay off and driving back home with Delilah. As they were preparing for bed, however, the phone rang and it was Kay. At her wit's end, Delilah grabbed the phone from E.V. and shouted at Kay to come on over because "we are going to have this over with." (Interestingly, what most incensed Kay about *Delilah* when it was published in 1981 had nothing to do with its revelations of her long affair with E.V. nor with her having provoked a showdown that led to E.V. and Delilah's divorce; it was the book's mentioning in passing that E.V. had given Delilah a venereal disease in the early years of the marriage while they were living in Youngstown, Ohio.)

After Kay had rushed over to Beech Lane in a cab, the three adults seated themselves in the large living room overlooking the woods and got down to business: "sometimes we were controlled, sometimes emotional," as *Delilah* records. At last the moment of truth arrived: "The hour was approaching two in the morning when we women decided my husband should choose between us; neither of us wanted to continue sharing him. I always thought that when the chips were down he would not leave his family; but he did. Slowly my husband strode across the living room, shook my hand, then went to her side."

What Delilah never knew was that her children had secretly witnessed the whole unfolding drama from the darkness at the top of the stairs. Having been "aroused by the declamatory tone of the grown-ups downstairs," Margie and Eddie sat on the top step holding hands and listening to their mother announce to E.V. and Kay that she and the children would go to live in a "little house in Texas" near her family. "This will be great!" Margie whispered to her brother, hoping that E.V. really would leave them because moving to Texas "sounded like fun." As the children looked on they saw their mother, now that E.V. had done the unthinkable and chosen Kay, walk over to the couple and with "eerie calm" give them each a kiss on the cheek. Graciously continuing to accept her defeat, Delilah asked of E.V. and Kay only that they "be sure to close the garage doors" as they drove off.

At this point, as Kay and E.V. took their leave, *Delilah*'s account would have it that Delilah experienced merely a "great sense of relief and calm" when they left. In reality, however, Delilah behaved quite differently. As soon as Kay and E.V. had departed for the Cadillac in the underground garage, Delilah went into hysterics. She rushed upstairs, found Margie, and frantically told her, "Margaret Anne, he's always loved you the most. You run out and stand in the driveway and our Daddy won't leave us if you do it." With Delilah now weeping and wailing in the doorway, Margie (who was in her nightgown) ran out into the snow and stood at the top of the driveway. "I can remember very clearly the headlights swinging around as he came out of the garage and headed up the driveway. And of course he stopped. I think he was swearing at Mother about what a cheap trick it was."

But after only a moment's pause E.V. drove off into the night with Kay. He would not be coming back.

Two

The Three Musketeers

Children love great occasions, including emergencies, and during the exciting night their father left them for Kay both Margie and Eddie were thrilled by the prospect of change and a move to a new city. After their father had driven off with Kay, Margie and Eddie joined Delilah on their parents' bed: "It seemed weird to sleep in their bed, but we all three huddled together," Margie remembers. It didn't take long for the darker side to their new life to set in, however, as the two children watched their mother struggling not to go to pieces. That Sunday the three of them sat in a pew in their Christian Science church and Margie felt "mortified that Mother was crying in church. She was just a wreck for years—she started calling us 'the Three Musketeers.'"

By dubbing them the Three Musketeers ("All for one and one for all") Delilah was doing her best to put an uplifting, even heroic, face on their new life together: she preferred to see herself "not only as a victim, but as a very noble victim." In their life as it was actually lived, however, what Delilah ended up imparting to her children was her shame and despair as well as the sense that they all had a share in the blame for the divorce. "It was never her problems with my father," Margie recalls, "it was always 'Daddy left us.'" Delilah inculcated this sense of shared blame so thoroughly that even today Ed will say "after we got divorced when I was seven," and Margie "when Daddy divorced us." And so while Delilah had officially declared that from this point on the Three Musketeers would "re-group and become this threesome that can conquer the world," what actually ended up happening is that she started drinking heavily.

Delilah began to feel so "lonely and afraid in the house on Beech Lane" that, just weeks after E.V. had moved out early in 1947, she decided she too would pull up stakes, installing herself and the children in "the charming Mariemont Inn," a mock-Tudor hotel in the leafy, deserted-looking Cincinnati suburb of Mariemont. It was the beginning of a pattern Delilah would hold to for the rest of her life: in times of trouble she would seek refuge in hotels. In fact, in these early years following the divorce Delilah and the children would live, with the exception of a year in a rented house in Texas near Delilah's family, in a succession of expensive hotels.

To help pick up her spirits Delilah had gone out and bought herself a fur coat, a diamond ring, and a Packard convertible that she named "Gertrude." Moreover, one exciting spring day while the divorce was still pending Delilah decided that she and the children would all benefit from a spur-of-the-moment vacation. Pulling up in Gertrude outside Hyde Park School and honking the special family signal (*honk! honk! honk-honk-honk!*), Delilah called out to her surprised children as they came running out, "Kids, I've got the car all packed and we're going to Florida!" That Delilah could just drive off with them in the middle of the school week was, for seven-year-old Eddie, a miraculous example of adult power—in the wink of an eye the homework assignment he'd been worrying about had been rendered meaningless.

Eddie did his part to pick up his mother's spirits after the divorce. One day he said to Delilah, "This is the X-A, Mother." "Whatever do you mean, dear?" she asked. "Well," he replied, "*X* is near the end of something and *A* is the beginning of something new." Delilah was so delighted by this tag for what they were going through that she wrote it down and the name stuck. For years afterward the Three Musketeers would refer to these early years following the divorce as the X-A, although Delilah somehow managed to get the meaning of the X-A backwards, thinking that *X* stood for "the approaching end" and *A* for "earlier, more happy times"—a quite different and gloomy interpretation.

For Margie, too, the X-A represented more an end than a beginning. What she would later see as the "good" part of her childhood had already come to a close the previous year when she'd been pulled out of Miss Doherty's (where she'd been a student, beginning at age three, for seven years) because E.V. declared that private school was making her "too uppity." She was enrolled (along with Eddie, who had entered kindergarten) at Hyde Park School, the local elementary school. Her fall from a golden childhood world was completed a year later when the divorce stripped her of her father, "the only parent I thought I had." The rest of her childhood and adolescence would be lived in relative misery.

If to no one else in the family, the original definition of the X-A clearly did apply to Eddie's own situation: the divorce brought an end to his isolation within the family and began a new and intense relationship with his mother. But while it was clear to Eddie's cousin Jean White, for example, that it was Margie, not Eddie, who was bitterly upset about the divorce, Delilah failed to grasp this. In fact, her giving the X-A her own altogether different meaning can be seen as symptomatic of her fundamental misreading of what was truly going on in her son at this time. In Delilah's mind Eddie was hit hardest of all by the divorce because, unlike Margie, he had never "received a lot of good basic fathering."

> One day, in driving past the Hyde Park School at afternoon recess, I saw Eddie sitting very close to the principal on the sidewalk curb. Then, day after day, after school he went to one of Mariemont's churches to talk to the minister. He was obviously seeking male companionship and counsel.

In Delilah's view, the key to understanding Eddie's mental state was the "wounds" she felt had been inflicted on him by the "loss" of E.V. (in *Delilah* the young Eddie is portrayed as sharing in the family mood exemplified by Margie's cry of "I want my daddy"). As Delilah saw it, underlying both Eddie's seeking out new father figures and his tormented feeling of having had a hand in causing the divorce was his grief over losing his father. It's not clear whether Delilah came to this belief through her training in child psychology, or because she herself was in mourning over

E.V.'s departure and assumed Eddie felt the same way, but the truth is that Eddie felt only relief at being rid of his father and his "scary, volcanic presence." Furthermore, Eddie's guilt about having set in motion his father's affair with Kay Beard was not a conclusion he'd reached on his own, but rather one that Delilah herself had started drumming into him by pointing out the apparently direct connection between his birth and E.V.'s taking up with Kay.

What Eddie found disturbing about the divorce was simply that his mother was going to pieces over it. Since the night E.V. had left them, Delilah had taken to telling her little son: "If I could only meet a man like you I would marry him," and "You alone understand me"—something Eddie found to be "a very big burden." Indeed, his mother's frequent crying spells and her voracious need to be comforted by him had imposed the "tremendous pressure" of trying to be a "parenting figure" himself. It was the need for "some sort of absolution" from the terrible strain of feeling responsible for his mother's anguish yet powerless to help her that drove Eddie to see the Mariemont minister (and it was just one visit, not several). Unfortunately, the well-meaning minister jumped to the pat conclusion that for Eddie the burning issue must be a desire to bring his parents back together (a supposition that Eddie was too shy to contradict) and Eddie left the church unsatisfied.

These feelings were what provoked Eddie's fit of hysteria back at the Mariemont Inn when, as *Delilah* recounts, "It took two hotel porters to help me hold that writhing, jumping little boy. As we held him tightly against the mattress of the bed, he began to relax and to cry out, 'I did it; I did it; it started because I was born!'" Ed remembers that he'd originally locked himself into the public toilet down the hall from their room—"I think they had to get the door taken off."

Ironically, both "experts"—the minister and Delilah with her new degree in child psychology—had failed to uncover Eddie's true feelings and thus be of any help at all.

Eddie's new and intense relationship with Delilah was very much a mixed blessing. Mixed, because there were also obvious benefits to being the new "man in her life" ("He was the man in her life," Margie recalls. "If she said that once, she said it a million times"). For if the effect of family life up until this point had been to make Eddie feel—already in his short life—a loss of faith in people so profound that he felt disassociated from the human race, now that he was the apple of his mother's eye Delilah "would just be sitting there moony-eyed when he was explaining something from his school," Margie remembers. Eddie for his part grew so devoted to her that "When she cried I became frantic and held on to her until she stopped. I wanted her to be happy, and I saved up money to buy her presents; if the gifts were ignored I felt powerless and dejected." The bond between mother and son grew so deep, in fact, that when Eddie was ten or eleven he told Delilah that if she died he would kill himself—a declaration that Delilah never forgot and would ever after quote back to him.

Still, the years of being virtually ignored at Beech Lane had created a little boy who'd learned to be quite independent and self-sufficient and Eddie "never had that little lamb-like desire to come up to the ewe and nestle against it." Moreover, Eddie's feelings for his mother would always be deeply ambivalent: "Whereas I loved her I dreaded her mysterious influence, as though she were a plant like rhubarb, stalk nourishing, leaves poisonous." And despite their new closeness, he couldn't help suspecting at times that his mother "had this announced and stated interest in me but that it was very peculiar in that it was very unperceiving. I felt like when I could be useful to her then she paid attention, but otherwise not." Even the tremendous pride Delilah took in her son's accomplishments can be seen, given her frequently stated desire to write a book entitled *How to Raise a Genius*, as something she enjoyed feeling because she could arrogate the credit to her own glorious mothering.

Delilah had divided feelings of her own about her new relationship with her son. On the one hand she'd begun telling him that the two of them shared "a perfect communication," that he, while only a little boy, was "far more mature than the riffraff she was dating," and that if the two of them didn't happen to be mother and son they surely would have been best friends or even gotten married. On the other hand Delilah often worried aloud that without "a suitable male role model" around him Eddie was "in danger of developing abnormally" and becoming an effeminate mama's boy. If for this reason alone, she would tell him, she hoped to remarry as soon as possible.

Thus seven-year-old Eddie, who'd recently learned by way of the divorce that he had a life, was now also learning how extremely changeable a life could be. For in the space of just a few months he'd gone from seeing so little of his mother that she hadn't been quite real to him to suddenly feeling almost married to her and her despair.

Having "researched the best area to which to move to give my children maximum educational advantages," Delilah found that "The answer was Evanston, Illinois. The school system was excellent; the town was in close proximity to Chicago with its many cultural activities; and it enjoyed the influence of Northwestern University." Delilah and the children moved to Evanston—a city of elms and churches with a history of integrated schools and liberal politics—in time for the 1947/48 school year and, as Eddie personally discovered as a second grader at Evanston's Miller Elementary School, the school system really was excellent.

In fact, Ed credits Miller Elementary School and its practice of progressive education as based on the writings of the philosopher John Dewey with transforming him from a boy who "started off as a stutterer and then went on to become somebody who spoke easily and always happily." Under progressive education, students were encouraged to speak up and "make a contribution." There were no grades, "no sense of competition and its rigors," a policy that enabled students to "improvise and speak in public without any kind of punishment or shame involved if you made a mistake."

Delilah and the children were now living at Evanston's Georgian Hotel. Like their previous residence, the Mariemont Inn in Cincinnati, the Georgian offered the hushed, walnut interiors and soothingly civilized ambiance that only money can buy.

Delilah could just afford this luxury hotel life because in the divorce settlement she had been awarded both five hundred dollars a month in child support and alimony (a tidy sum in the late 1940s) as well as a lump sum of seven thousand dollars (E.V. having sold off a second, construction, business). Nonetheless, Delilah "was anguished about money and was always worrying that there wouldn't be enough and that Daddy would cut us off"—a fear that was to become "the major theme of the post-divorce childhood. There was this feeling that we were trained as little courtesans. 'Be nice to your father or he'll cut us off.'"

It's a testament to just how afraid Delilah was and always would be to live in a home of her own that she moved herself and the children into the Georgian even though the only accommodation available—room 205A—was a single furnished room with twin beds that required Margie and Eddie to take turns sleeping on the floor. This eccentric arrangement ended only several months later when a suite of rooms—a living room with a Murphy bed for Delilah, a bedroom that Margie and Eddie shared, and a kitchenette—opened up. Yet even after the family settled into the suite, Margie and Eddie continued to dine regularly in the Georgian's dining room with its "linen table cloths and waiters in fancy cummerbunds" because Delilah had taken to going out carousing in the evenings.

"My appetite for pleasure became insatiable," Delilah admits in her autobiography. "The nightclubs and supper clubs of Chicago tempted me, and I was far more popular with the smart set than I thought I would be." On the many occasions when Margie and Eddie dined alone in the hotel dining room they would occasionally take a measure of revenge against their mother by ordering the most expensive dish on the menu, with Margie playing pranks such as putting salt in the sugar bowl and Eddie making sure to give the waiter an extravagant tip. At other times, however, the two of them, never the best of friends, would sit at separate tables, each of them signing their own bill. Sometimes Margie would even avoid her brother altogether by dining at a different hour.

Delilah, whose approach to mothering was typically fluctuating and unstable, could never settle on a definitive role to play around her children and alternated between treating them as equals and wanting to be a more traditional disciplinarian. She was after all someone who managed for years to maintain simultaneous beliefs in both Christian Science and modern science. And Delilah can in fact be seen as several mothers. She was the wise mother who indulged her gifted son's passing enthusiasms for imported teas from Marshall Fields or for harp lessons (during their first year in Evanston, Delilah even enrolled in a class given on the Gifted Child at Northwestern University).

Yet as she gradually made her way into a career as a child psychologist,* Delilah was also a mother who couldn't resist giving psychological tests to her own children as well as to Margie's new best friend, Penny McLeod. Whether Rorschach, Stanford-Binet, TAT, the Picture Completion, or the House-Tree-Person, each time a new test appeared on the market Delilah would be sure to try it out on her "guinea pigs." Moreover, Delilah—who maintained "Edmund White" and "Margaret White" folders in her filing cabinet—never failed to tell her children the test results. Margie was informed, for example, that her I.Q. had been measured at 140, while Eddie was told that his was 170. After Delilah had given Eddie a Rorschach test, she told him frankly that she found it distressing he had failed to see any human beings in the inkblot designs (seven-year-old Eddie, who was now rather "spooky" in his detachment from people, had seen only "jewels, graveyards, and chandeliers").

Delilah was also by turns the busy single mother whose latchkey kids were left to fend for themselves as well as the suffering mother in need of comfort, even babying, from her young children. For absent as Delilah habitually was from home life at the Georgian Hotel, when she did spend an evening at home with her children she was often enough overwhelmingly needy. At times

---

* Delilah's professional career, which would culminate in her becoming the director of a clinic for the mentally retarded at Chicago's Cook County Hospital a few years later, began during this first year in Evanston when she worked as a teacher's assistant in the Evanston Public Schools during the 1947/48 school year.

Delilah would fall into complete despair in front of her children. More than once during this year at the Georgian, Delilah would suddenly threaten to jump out the window, telling them in a mournful and dramatic voice, "You know, children, I feel something drawing me to the ground." At these awful moments Margie would catch hold of her mother's blouse and plead with her not to jump. What's more, in these early days following the divorce, Delilah wrote E.V. a "Medea-like" letter threatening to drive herself and the children into Lake Michigan and drown them all if he didn't increase his child support payments.

Some of Delilah's suffering can be explained by her having been a "baby doll wife" who in all her years of marriage had been so shielded from practical concerns that she'd never written a check; now, with the divorce, she was forced in middle age to get a job for the first time and become an independent adult. Then too, E.V. was often on Delilah's mind and his loss was something she would continue to mourn and pick over for years to come. Yet despite the many feverish speculations Delilah made about the demise of the marriage, she never felt she'd gotten to the bottom of things and ended up conceding that E.V.'s mind would forever remain a mystery to her. It's characteristic of Delilah (who had a lifelong blind spot for unpleasant truths, particularly those involving herself) that none of her speculations involved any real shortcomings on her own part. It's also characteristic of her that she restlessly flitted among competing theories without ever reaching any conclusion. One of her theories was that E.V. hadn't been cut out for family life: "To have one child was one thing, but two constituted a family. It became more and more obvious he was not a family man." Another was that he had never loved her in the first place, as his "long history of infidelity" throughout their married life would seem to show. A third theory was that he'd viewed her not as a wife but as a mother figure. A fourth was that he deeply resented (or felt threatened by) her having gotten a master's degree (after all, he'd jokingly told her stepfather, "If she gets one more degree, I'm going to leave her"). Her fifth theory, however, saw the problem as lying not with her academic achievements but rather with his own success in business: "I read in my psychological studies that it takes more maturity to stand success than it does to stand failure. Perhaps my husband was such a case."

Of course, it didn't help matters that E.V.—the very antithesis of a "communicator"—never provided Delilah with a clear idea about why he left her and the children. Nevertheless, in the speculations in which she continued to indulge for the rest of her life Delilah never hit on what was almost certainly the real reason E.V. had become disenchanted with her—her attitude, as opposed to Kay's, regarding his business.

As a divorcée Delilah, who had torn to pieces the letter E.V. had written her in the summer of 1947 informing her of his upcoming marriage to Kay Beard, continued to get emotional each time she received E.V.'s monthly alimony and child support check because the mere sight of his handwriting could make her weep. And yet Delilah would have gladly forgotten all about E.V. if she could have found an appropriately well-off replacement. Her search for a new husband was impeded, however, by her being a woman deep in her forties with two kids in tow, as well as by her chubbiness. Delilah, who had first gained weight during and after her pregnancy with Eddie, had now become still heavier, reaching a peak of 168 pounds—a lot for a woman only five feet tall.

"How my mother longed for that phone to ring," Ed writes in *A Boy's Own Story* in a passage discussing her dating struggles. For while one night stands were something Delilah came by easily enough, it was the serious commitment she wanted from a man that was so difficult to find. The failure of her "brilliant, glittering black" telephone to ring is something that Ed, with characteristically cynical worldliness, sees as "proof of the inefficacy of yearning. No thought, no architecture of thoughts no matter how intricate, could make that phone ring. Only beauty, youth, charm, money—only those things worked. The rest (goodness, worthiness, the conjuring of desire) was a pitiable substitute for the brute fact of glamour."

In these early years following the divorce Margie suffered and languished almost as much as Delilah did. In fact, Margie's abiding feeling now that they'd entered the X-A (a feeling that Delilah must have privately shared) was that she and her mother and brother, far from being the Three Musketeers, had in fact become three losers. Even Eddie, who alone had benefited overall from the X-A, couldn't help but register this collective family shame—something that *A Boy's Own Story* vividly describes:

> *The great event of our household had been that my father had left us for someone else. Afterward, how could we like each other all that much, since we were all equally guilty of having driven him away? At least, we'd failed to keep him. Nor was our shared fate black as good ink or crisp as a crow's wing on snow; we hadn't been assigned clear, tragic roles we could play with any sort of despairing joy. Instead, we'd been shamed and we'd become vacant, neglected, shabby with neglect.*

But a further humiliation for Margie was that even within this forlorn trio she would always feel like a third wheel because Eddie and Delilah had taken to "fawning all over each other. She was hanging on him constantly after the divorce. It was sort of sickening, really. And of course that made me feel so left out and so angry." After all, the alignment spelled out in the "family mythology"—that Eddie was Delilah's child and Margie E.V.'s—hardly worked in Margie's favor now that E.V., who could be remote enough in person, was hundreds of miles away back in Cincinnati. Margie was forced to grow up with a mother so "male-oriented" that she honestly felt at times that Delilah esteemed the male family dog Timmy—"Mother's second son"—above Margie herself. "Anything that was a male she would ascribe these sensitive, intelligent qualities to. Anything that's female was stable, with her feet on the ground. Ed was brilliant—unique—and I was good old Margaret Anne, the salt of the earth, not very interesting but you can always count on her."

But even though Margie would jealously resent for years how Delilah favored Eddie, she also felt that overall both she and her brother were regarded by their divorced parents as being more of a nuisance than anything else: "we felt we were in everybody's way."

One notion of parenting that Delilah did practice consistently was sparing her children nothing.

Up until the time of my divorce I followed my mother's theory— spare children all unnecessary anxiety. Afterwards I questioned that rule. Had I myself been too shielded from life's ugly side? Was I too idealistic to cope with life's contingencies? Had my own upbringing led me to overprotect my children? In any event, when we were on our own, I chose the opposite tack. I took my children almost every place—to nightclubs, on tours to see the seamy side of Chicago and certainly on excursions to acquaint them with all types of handicapping conditions. I spared them practically nothing and in that way they became sophisticated. In a real sense the three of us learned together.

Delilah did indeed take her children everywhere. In fact, Eddie celebrated his eighth, ninth, and tenth birthdays at his mother's side in nightclubs: "She'd split a simple pasta dish with me to save money and then order highball after highball as we'd look longingly toward the man at the bar. Had he noticed Mother? Would he send her a drink? Or would he be scared off by my presence?" Delilah also kept little that was on her mind to herself. Indeed, she now recognized so few "boundaries" between herself and her children that, in one astounding example, she confided to eight-year-old Eddie that his father's penis had been surprisingly small. That Delilah was "exposing Eddie too much to what was going on" was apparent to Delilah's former sister-in-law Helen White, who also felt concerned that Delilah was burdening him with her troubles.

What is striking even in the province of autobiography, where it's always a temptation to improve one's past, is how thoroughly Delilah has rewritten her conduct as a mother and its effect on her children. In *Delilah*, her neglect of them before the divorce is recast into her having shielded them from the terrible state of their parents' marriage; and what had often been her shameless and self-centered lack of all restraint after the divorce is transformed into a wise nurturing of worldliness in them. For all this,

Ed today generously explains away the failures and excesses of his mother's parenting as having been caused by the lack of established role models available to a divorced professional woman with children in the middle America of the 1940s. He points out that Delilah was someone who had had to improvise her way, without any real guidance, through major transitions in social class, locale, and mode of life—from an impoverished childhood in rural Texas, to an upper-middle-class life in Cincinnati as E.V.'s wife, to a career as a psychologist.

A fuller and more objective view of Delilah, however, would suggest that at least part of the blame for her erratic and flawed parenting must be laid on her own personal weaknesses. As much as she certainly suffered in the years before and after the divorce, and granted that she was attempting to navigate the lives of herself and her children in an era when neither divorcées nor professional women were commonplace (even in relatively enlightened Evanston there was still a whiff of scandal to divorce), the fact remains that Delilah underwent these wrenching transitions amidst elegant surroundings and pampered herself all along the way with heavy drinking and heavy reliance on her children, particularly Eddie.

In any event, the lack of an established model for how to live the life of a divorced professional woman with children did lead Delilah to decide (after a year in Evanston) to move herself and the children to Dallas, Texas for the 1948/49 school year. "My parents were fearful that I could not rear the children alone and continued to urge me to move to Texas to be near my family," she wrote in her autobiography. "Their insistence further eroded my self-confidence, and I yielded to them, despite the fact that the Evanston schools had offered me full-time employment in the psychology department with a good salary for the coming year."

Not surprisingly, perhaps, moving to "Big D," as Dallas is still sometimes known, proved to be a big mistake. As it turned out, Delilah and the children never felt "particularly at home in Texas," nor did they see much of Delilah's parents—their reason for coming to Texas in the first place. Delilah's mother Willie Loula and stepfather Robert Lee Snider lived 120 miles from

Dallas in Ranger, Texas (not far from Stephenville, Delilah's birthplace) where "Mr. Snahder," as the locals and even his wife called him, was the head of the math department—the only one in the department, in fact—at Ranger Junior College. Because no suitable hotel could be found, Delilah put aside her fears of living in a house and settled herself and the children in a rented bungalow in Preston Hollow, a subdivision on the outskirts of Dallas that was still so new at the time, much of it was raw fields. Delilah would later put a brave face on this miserable year by calling it, in a letter to E.V., a "sojourn in Texas with family, roses, and sunshine," but the only good that seems to have come from the year in Dallas was Delilah's accidental discovery of what would eventually become her calling in psychology: working with the handicapped.

Otherwise, Delilah, Margie, and Eddie all suffered in Big D. Delilah discovered that Dallas was "a city for couples" and that single women were not welcome in the better restaurants, such as the one in the Baker Hotel (it was assumed single women could only be up to no good). Margie was bitten so badly by a tarantula that crawled up from the floorboards one night that her wound would eventually require surgery. And Eddie was bitterly unhappy in his new school. Having learned that a life could be changed, Eddie would continue to learn in these restless early years following the divorce just what tremendous change could be brought to his year-by-year fortunes. Attending third grade at the more traditional and repressive public school in Dallas, particularly after his year of progressive education in Evanston, was a "tremendous shock" to him; among other things, his hands were "beat with a ruler because I talked too much." *Delilah* recounts a still more painful experience that befell Eddie at school this year:

It was during this year that the loneliness of the gifted child struck me. One day Eddie came in from school crying hysterically. Nothing quieted him as he rolled on the bed burying his face in his hands. His unrestrained grieving went on and on until finally, when he became quiet enough to talk, he told me that a little boy had come to school and shown everyone his new knife except him. This outright rejection was more than he could bear. I was unable to comfort him, since my own rejection was still all too new.

Finding himself isolated in this alien, even hostile, world, Eddie insulated himself by retreating into fantasies just as he had done at age four when he'd spent a year at home alone—with the difference being that now he was "older and nuttier." For at age eight in Dallas, Eddie was no longer imagining friends that were irritatingly vague and unreal, but imagining—and believing—himself to be a god: "At last the imagination, like a mold on an orange, was covering the globe of my mind."

If the imaginary playmates he'd invented four years before were an example of the exaggerated consolations of the imagination, Eddie's going off the deep end in Dallas can be seen as a striking demonstration of the powerful *exaggerations* of the imagination. His "delusions of grandeur" reached such a pitch during this year he convinced himself that he wielded magic powers. Among other things, he believed these powers he possessed allowed him, with a special shake of his fingers, to influence the "big storms that would sweep in across the fields. I felt I could control them— the lightning and thunder." Another favorite fantasy was that he had died. As people gathered around his tomb during the funeral, he would suddenly "wake up and frighten them all."

When Eddie wasn't fantasizing that he was a god, he was imagining he was a king. In fact, from now on his boyhood imagination would be marked by a persistent theme of royalty and toward this end he'd invented a game in Dallas that he called "King and Slave."

The only people around to enlist in the game were Margie and their two cousins, Sue and Jean White (who also lived in the area), the pretty daughters of E.V.'s younger brother Bill and his wife Helen. As Ed remembers it, "I would oftentimes play the slave because what seemed important to me was that the rituals be conducted properly and that deference be shown to the king. Nobody else seemed to get it right—they didn't know how to do it and they didn't seem to care enough—and I was very good at being either slavish or kingly. But it was almost more important that the whole thing be acted out than that I play any particular role. But I do think that the payoff was supposed to be that if I was a very good slave for hours and hours, then I could get to be the king and then I would have shown them through my own example how to be a good slave."

Interestingly, none of the other players of "King and Slave" has any recollection of Ed's playing any role other than the king. Jean White remembers that at his urging the four children would create castles by draping sheets over furniture and then, always assuming the role of king, Eddie would "script everything out and direct everyone." Margie found the whole game so boring that all she remembers of it is that Eddie would make a royal entrance wearing a paper or cardboard crown, "wind himself up in the living room drapes" and give inadvertent glimpses of "his little skinny bare chest." To his credit, however, Eddie was always a benevolent king who never bullied or ordered anybody around: "I'm not sure he even really needed us—he was very taken with the whole drama." Sure enough, Eddie was quite content to enact royal proceedings and processions on his own, arranging tea boxes in such a way as to create palaces and court-yards and avenues and then imagining crowds of "little people all cheering the entrance of the king."

Helen White was also aware of her nephew's penchant for playacting the role of king during this year in Dallas. Helen, who would sometimes look after Eddie for whole weekends when Delilah and Margie went off to visit Delilah's parents by them-selves, found him to be a well-mannered, precocious, and "extra-intelligent" little boy. On Sundays, for instance, she would first deposit her own two children at the Baptist Sunday School and then, at Eddie's insistence, take him with her to the adult church service where he would be very fidgety as he sat beside her in the pew—not out of boredom but rather from being "overeager to see and hear everything going on" around him. One weekend Helen gave him a book of mythology and Eddie exclaimed, "Aunt Helen, I just love the gods and goddesses!"

The persistent theme of royalty began to show up in the plays that Eddie had started writing. During this year in Dallas he wrote his first play, *The Blue Bird*, a play in three acts that he'd based on a fairy tale of the same name ("my first effort in plagiarism"). When his school failed to show any interest in putting the play on, Delilah charged into action, attending a local PTA meeting and insisting that her son's play be produced. The result was that *The Blue Bird* was staged after all ("a big success," as *Delilah* notes triumphantly), with Eddie himself playing the lead and wearing a splendid king costume Delilah had rented from a professional costumer's. *The Blue Bird* was only the first of several class plays Eddie would write that invariably featured a royal role for himself. In fourth grade he wrote *The Death of Hector* (Prince Hector, Priam's oldest son, was a Trojan hero in Homer's *Iliad* slain by Achilles), and in fifth or sixth grade, Eddie played the role of Charles VII in a play he and some classmates improvised on the story of Joan of Arc ("a weak king who is helped out by this sort of tom-boyish lesbian girl" is the story line that eventually emerged). Finally, during the summer he was twelve Ed staged *Boris Godounov* at summer camp. "The whole point of all these plays was just so that I could make big entrances and exits as a king" (when everyone would bow to him). "That was the only thing I was interested in."

To a lesser but surprising degree, Ed's adult imagination has continued to be occupied with royal fantasies—in fact, the desire to be a king would emerge as a psychological "throughline" in his life. In his first published novel, *Forgetting Elena*, the narrator ultimately discovers that he is a prince and part of the royal Valentine line (something that harks back to Ed's being, in real life, "the seventh Valentine in the White descent," as Delilah once grandly put it). In Ed's personal life, two revelations of how close to his heart these royal fantasies have remained came to the surface during widely spaced therapy sessions. In the first instance, Ed was attending a weekend marathon of group therapy in the 1970s during which each person was asked to act out his deepest fantasy; when Ed's turn came up he found that "again, mine was that I was a king." In the mid-1990s Ed was asked by his latest therapist why he seemed to feel no rage about AIDS; Ed's answer (which surprised himself as well as his therapist) was that "I always wanted to be a king and now I am one."

Amusingly, Ed—the author of *Nocturnes for the King of Naples*—was once actually mistaken for a king while visiting Naples. Having finished a meal at a Naples restaurant with his friend Marie-Claude de Brunhoff, Ed pulled out his American Express card (which read Edmund Valentine White III) and went off to the men's room. The restaurant's owner, meanwhile, unfamiliar with the pompous American practice of adding a III or IV to the names of sons in the manner of royal families, came to the table and "asked Marie-Claude if I was a king. And Marie-Claude said, 'Shhhh,' as though I were, but was traveling anonymously."

At the end of 1948 the Three Musketeers drove from Dallas to Kentucky to spend the holidays with Delilah's current boyfriend, Greg. A dashing, much-younger man who'd been a fighter pilot in World War II and was also recently divorced, Greg was someone Delilah had met the year before through friends in Cincinnati. On Christmas Day, Greg announced to Margie and Eddie: "I'm a poor man but my Christmas present to you and your mother is I'm going to marry your mother." While Margie was thrilled, Eddie was appalled by the prospect of a "cornball" and "fly-by-night drunk" stepfather, the "kind of macho monster who didn't even have Daddy's virtues of being solid and dependable and rich."

What ended up horrifying Margie was Delilah's behavior a week later, on New Year's Eve. Delilah and Greg had tucked Margie and Eddie into "these bunk beds," telling them, "We'll see you in the morning. We'll be in the kitchen washing the dishes." At midnight, however, the children were awakened by firecrackers and bells celebrating the new year; padding out into the kitchen, they discovered they were alone in the house. Twelve-year-old Margie panicked and thought, "I must call the police and tell them that my mother has disappeared." But then Margie realized that she had no idea where they were—she'd never learned Greg's address. Eddie started crying and Margie cleaned his face with a washrag. When she did finally call the police they instructed her to go outside and read the street sign and house number. Just as the squad car arrived, "Greg and Mother showed up, drunk" (they'd been celebrating in a nearby tavern). When the police left the scene, Delilah beat Margie "within an inch of my life," shouting at her, "How dare you call the police!"

Soon afterwards Delilah and Greg's engagement was abruptly broken off (he'd been after her to buy him a fishing camp, for one thing), and on the long drive home to Dallas Delilah tormented herself aloud with her endlessly shifting (but ultimately circular) thoughts about Greg. It disturbed and confused Margie to see her mother so "cuckoo," declaring in rapid succession, "He's not right for me"; "I'm going to marry him"; and then back to "He's not right for me" (the decision she stuck to in the end). As the miles flew by Delilah's thoughts swung back to her ex-husband, a theme vividly reconstructed in *A Boy's Own Story*:

> *Mother started reciting the litany of our lives. She questioned us once more about our father and how he behaved toward his new wife. Each twisted or colored fact we gave her she plaited into a heavy weave. Then she tore that up and started again. He would soon leave his wife or he would never leave her, he was being blackmailed by that woman, no he loved her, he was a man of honor, no he was a man without principle, he had failed us, no he stayed true, he'd tire of her, no she was a born fascinator, this was just an adventure, it was a life, she made him feel superior, she made him feel cheap, he'd soon be back or he'd never return....*

As she drove along, Delilah would take frequent nips from her "whikey," as she called the flask of whisky she kept in the glove compartment. When Gertrude the car would start weaving off the highway onto the gravel shoulder, Margie would plead with her mother to stop drinking but Delilah would snap, "No smart mouth kid's going to tell me what to do." As night fell the mood in the car softened, and Margie and Eddie would each take a turn lying on the front seat with their head in Delilah's lap. To soothe themselves, all three would sing: "There's a long, long trail a-winding...."

On these long trips, the family would stop for the night at

"these drafty, high-ceilinged hotels with a transom over the door." Delilah would tell them: "You know, these places are just firetraps, kids. Now I'm going to open the transom but we must have our hotel manners and you must be quiet." Yet having warned them of the firetrap they were staying in, Delilah was soon leaving the children alone in the room to go out on the town for the evening. Margie believes that such experiences contributed to her and Eddie's "deep fear of abandonment" because they so often had no idea where Delilah had gone to or when or if she would be coming back.

Although Eddie and especially Margie were to have several run-ins with their combustible stepmother, E.V.'s marriage to Kay in August of 1947—a bare two months or so after the divorce had gone through—had the virtue of at least establishing some kind of home for the children to visit. For when Margie and Eddie visited their father that first summer before his remarriage, E.V. was living in a rooming house by himself where his methods for looking after the kids included parking them at a movie theater near his downtown office for four consecutive showings of *Key Largo*.

That summer E.V. also took Eddie and Margie horseback riding at Clifty Falls State Park—an experience that provides a vivid example of the intimidating power of E.V.'s personality. E.V. was an excellent horseman who as an adolescent had been a cowhand on his uncle's ranch where he shot rattlesnakes "with a pistol when they'd get in bed with him to stay warm." After saddling the horses at Clifty Falls State Park, E.V.—with a cigar clenched in his small, tobacco-stained teeth and wearing his "ridiculous straw hat"—bellowed out "Hi ho, Texas!" and left his terrified children behind in the dust. "Daddy would just go tearing down these hills, breakneck speed, thundering downhill," Margie recalls. "You know, it's scary to ride a horse downhill in the woods. He was showing off, of course. Ed and I would just be, 'Oh, my god.'" E.V.'s constant cigar meant that "you could still smell him" even after he'd charged off into the distance.

Because E.V. insisted that they ride all day long, the following morning Margie and Eddie would be so sore they could hardly walk.

Following E.V. and Kay's marriage, each August when Margie and Eddie would go off to visit their father and stepmother for the month, Delilah would make them feel as though they were "spies" being sent behind enemy lines. Because Delilah had still not given up hope that E.V. might return to her, she expected her children to be on the lookout for any possible signs of discord between Kay and E.V. On the other hand, in keeping with Delilah's ongoing anxiety that E.V. might cut them off financially, Delilah would also hand the children a list of topics—to be memorized on the train en route to Cincinnati—that Margie and Eddie were forbidden to discuss. Forbidden topics included such information as Delilah's having sold the Mullet Lake summer house, or having bought a new car. "We had to make it sound as though we were barely getting by," Margie recalls.

On these summer visits Margie and Eddie were a study in contrasts. While Margie was "more principled" and honored Delilah's forbidden topics with her silence, Eddie was "a total hypocrite" always ready to start "betraying Mummie" by supplying forbidden information whenever the opportunity arose in conversation to score points with E.V. and Kay. And while Margie was cold to Kay and "feudal in her loyalty to Mother," Eddie was a smooth and shameless flatterer of his stepmother. Although he'd been babying and buttering up his mother since he was three, Eddie would turn on his charm even more brightly around his stepmother because he was afraid of her, showering her with compliments such as, "Oh Kay, you look so delightful. Your nails are so beautiful." Just as he would do at home with Delilah, Eddie would often read books aloud to Kay—something that made Margie "want to throw up. I was so mad those days at him."

While admitting today that he had been a devious and disloyal charmer, Ed maintains that "I felt like whoever I was with I had to court in order to survive." The flip side to his precociously cynical sense that people's love, even his family's love, was so provisional that it was always threatening to dry up if not freshly flattered, was his own very shallow sense of allegiance. Eddie's early feeling of alienation from the human race, of having been let down by it, had left him "ready to betray anybody." Yet putting it this way ignores the lighter side of Ed's compulsion to continually court the people around him—the simple pleasure he took (and still takes today) in pleasing. As any experienced courtier knows, the full exercise of charm requires that one devote oneself entirely to the people at hand, unhindered by any principles—particularly loyalty.

Far from trying to charm or flatter her new stepmother, Margie often didn't bother to hide her contempt—something that further antagonized the naturally volatile Kay. In Margie's eyes, Kay was a "hick" who "in a lot of ways wasn't very polished." In fact, Margie believes that one reason her father preferred Kay over Delilah was that Kay "would yell right back at him, whereas Mother would cry and he would feel guilty." Kay in this view was more a peer, someone who resembled E.V. in being able to "go from being fine-mannered and dignified to being just the most base of persons."

Yet in the opinion of George Newman, the son of Kay and E.V.'s next-door neighbors and someone who—as will be seen—got to know Kay and E.V. as a couple better than anyone, Kay succeeded as a wife to E.V. because she recognized that her husband was a "kind of prima donna" who demanded that those close to him do "what he wanted to do, when he wanted to do it." Kay was thus at great pains to indulge his whims and bend to his eccentric schedule—whether this meant working by his side throughout the night at the office, accompanying him for a midnight dinner out, or rising at three in the afternoon to see to his breakfast. Kay also "never did anything that E.V. didn't want done." This spirit of accommodation fit neatly into another strategy on Kay's part: her determination not to "let him out of her sight any more than she had to" (a very sensible strategy given that Kay herself had been the other woman in E.V.'s life for several years).

Helen White, whose daughters Sue and Jean lived with Kay and E.V. for a time after their father, E.V.'s younger brother Bill, suffered a stroke, noticed that while Kay was "good" to Helen's own daughters and to Eddie, Kay and Margie never got along well. Indeed, Margie tangled with Kay more than once, one dramatic example being the summer Margie and Eddie arrived in Cincinnati only to find Kay (who could be very stingy, something that can be attributed to her having grown up a poor farmer's daughter) erupting because her two "terribly spoiled" stepchildren had taken the train as usual instead of the much cheaper bus. E.V. joined the fray and things escalated to the point where he and Kay "just became crazed." When Margie ran to the telephone to call Delilah, Kay ripped the phone out of her hands and wrapped the cord around Margie's neck, actually starting to strangle her. Afterwards, Margie and Eddie "half-kiddingly and half-seriously" sat around plotting how they might kill their wicked stepmother.

Eddie's devious charm had little or no effect on his father, who was essentially charm-proof—at least to the charms of a disappointing and sissy son. Then again, much of Eddie and Margie's relationship with their father centered around the yard work (or "yard-life" as he once memorably termed it) that he assigned them. And while Margie's work ethic earned E.V.'s grudging respect ("The things my father valued the most about me were very masculine traits," Margie remembers, such as her leadership, athleticism, and even her gumption in standing up for her mother and what she believed in), E.V. regarded Eddie as a hopeless and "horrible worker" who was doomed to end up a failure much like E.V.'s brother Bill, whom E.V. sometimes privately referred to as "The Failure." E.V. would assign the two children the task of raking his large yard, for example, and Margie "would just work like a little Trojan to please him," while Eddie, as soon as his father's back was turned, would "sit behind a tree and read a book."

Another task was cleaning the gutters—something E.V. "had this big thing about" (he could often be seen atop a tall ladder, a cigar in his mouth, methodically doing the job himself). But while Margie cleaned the gutters as diligently as her father, Eddie would get squeamish about getting his hands in muck and "go 'ooh!'" Whatever task Eddie had been assigned, the end result was almost always that E.V. would berate him for being a quitter: "You're never going to amount to anything, goddamn it, you never finish what you start." E.V. would remain unwavering in his conviction that his son was doomed to failure even after Ed had moved to New York upon graduating college, had his prizewinning play produced off-Broadway, and landed an editorial position at Time-Life. Perhaps E.V., whose own success was due in large part to hard work and a disciplined, "grin and bear it" approach to the drudgery of unpleasant tasks, found it impossible to imagine anything but a poor future for someone with such bad work habits regarding the gutters.

In any event, it's no great surprise that Ed now finds he has "a terrible amnesia for that period because it was all so unpleasant."

As an adult Margie learned to despair of ever depicting the family relationships in all their complexity to "all the poor therapists I had." For beneath the simple dichotomy spelled out in the family mythology—that Eddie was Delilah's child, and Margie E.V.'s—flowed more subtle undercurrents. For instance, "her" parent, E.V., would make "lewd, lurid, mean comments" about Delilah, and Margie would feel obliged to fly to Delilah's defense "because I felt she had no one else" to stick up for her (her "phony" little brother being of no help). "I don't think Mother ever understood what I went through to defend her to Daddy, and yet she loved Eddie more." And though Margie loved her father, E.V. could be a "horrible, very cruel man." At the dinner table he could let fly with outrageously provocative slurs about Delilah: "Well, you know kids, your mother never was very faithful. On our wedding night she was out shackin' up with some young fella." Still more painfully, E.V. would link Margie to Delilah in his attacks, telling Margie "You're just like your mother—you smell bad and you cry all the time."

Having sung Kay's praises, betrayed Delilah's confidence by openly blabbing about every item on the list of forbidden topics, and failed to rally behind Margie in defending their mother, Eddie would return home and immediately start "sucking up" to Delilah once more, acting scandalized by all the terrible things Kay and E.V. had said about her. It's a weakness that Margie still recognizes in her brother today. "He charms everyone he's with but then he turns around and talks about you behind your back."

Things were going so dismally in Dallas that Delilah (who had lined up a new job back in Illinois as an area psychologist for the State Department of Education) impulsively whisked her children off on a long car trip weeks before school let out, much as she'd cheered them all up a few years earlier by taking them to Florida while school was still in session.

Unfortunately, Delilah's new job was not in the Chicago area, as she'd hoped, but in Rockford—a much smaller city in northern Illinois about an hour's drive from Chicago. As the 1949/50 school year began Delilah and the children once again took up quarters in a hotel, this time in a suite of rooms at Rockford's Faust Hotel. Like the Mariemont Inn and the Georgian, the Faust was "the fanciest hotel," as Margie remembers—"it took all of our money." After the horrors of third grade in Dallas, Eddie's year in Rockford at the Keith Country Day School was relatively upbeat. And while Keith Country Day did not feature the Dewey-ite progressive education that Eddie had come to love at Miller Elementary School in Evanston, it did have the small classes and respect for the arts befitting an indulgent private school. Perhaps it was the awful time Eddie had had at the public school in Dallas that led Delilah to enroll him in a private school. In any event, Margie was sent to the local public junior high school in Rockford—an experience she calls "the most miserable year in my life."

The first draft of a lengthy and important letter from Delilah to E.V., written from the Faust Hotel early in 1950, reveals that while spending Christmas of 1949 with his father in Cincinnati nine-year-old Eddie had caused E.V. such concern with his compulsive habit of bobbing his head that E.V. had written Delilah wondering if their son might not have some undetected neurological damage. This head-bobbing, what Ed now calls "the neck thing," is something that "tortured me for years"—so much so that he dreaded going to movie theaters because so often the people sitting behind him would complain that his head-bobbing obscured their view. The problem would continue to plague him into early adulthood.

Delilah's letter to E.V. establishes how surprisingly early on it was that E.V. first became alarmed about his son—a sense of alarm that, during Ed's adolescence, would grow into a major theme. It also shows how this rare personal word from E.V. provided Delilah with her first opportunity in the three years since the divorce (what she delicately refers to as her and the children's "road to readjustment") to discuss intimate family matters with him. For along with the letter's official message of reassurance (Delilah tells him their son's problems are not "physical, but rather psychological," and that E.V. should "not worry, because I do not believe he is seriously disturbed"), Delilah is unable to resist making her letter into a reproach to a much-missed ex-husband, a sort of state of the family address on the brave struggles of the Three Musketeers who have been heartlessly cast out into the world by him.

Delilah begins her letter by subtly reprimanding E.V. for his remoteness as a father: "Your letter came today and I shall answer it right away as Eddie's problems have been of serious concern to me for a long time." Although she hastens to assure E.V. that "my remarks are not intended to be condemnatory, but just facts as I see them as a mother and a child psychologist," in fact what has clearly started percolating below the surface between Delilah and E.V is a battle of perceptions as to who is more to blame for their son's personal problems. In Delilah's view of things, the "nervous mannerisms" (which she summarizes as "eye-blinking, head bobbing, hand twisting, stuttering, etc.") that E.V. had been so alarmed to observe in their son over Christmas can be attributed both to the effects of the divorce as well as to Eddie's "native inheritance."

> *Eddie was predetermined to nervousness in his basic neurological structure as evidenced by a convulsion* [following his birth] *before leaving the hospital, and severe tantrums at a very early age due to tension, and frequent crying spells.... Environmentally, Eddie is the victim of a broken home, and while all children suffer under these circumstances, the intellectually and emotionally exceptional child is doomed to far more suffering due to the greater sensitiveness.*
>
> *... I work with behavior problems every day and at the top of the list of causes for disturbances are broken homes, so I am fairly well acquainted with the problem and our children, unfortunately, have not been spared regardless of my knowledge of the situation because it is not a thing of the mind, but of the emotions.*

By declaring divorce and a naturally nervous disposition to be responsible for their son's "present condition," Delilah seems to be refuting any notion that her own mothering may also be to blame. For the divorce is something about which E.V. did feel defensive, if not guilty. E.V. had in fact strongly resisted the idea of divorce (after all, it had been Delilah and Kay who forced him to choose between them) and even on the day they were filing for divorce E.V. was proposing to Delilah a kind of continental arrangement whereby they would remain married but he would be allowed to keep Kay on as his mistress. After the divorce had gone through E.V. would ever after regard it as a mistake, not so much because of the pain he'd caused Delilah and the children but because it constituted what he felt was the only real stain on his moral record—the one aspect of his life, that is, that someone from his set and class could point to as being an indefensible transgression. Delilah, for her part, came to regret agreeing to the divorce—and not just for what it seemed to have done to the children. She too felt stung by the disgrace of divorce but her long years as a divorcée, more painful and difficult than she could ever have foreseen (for one thing, she'd imagined a second marriage), left her thinking later in life that accepting E.V.'s offer to stay married but keep Kay might have been the best choice after all, humiliating as that had seemed at the time.

Having distanced herself from blame, Delilah turns to rehabilitating Eddie's image in E.V.'s eyes:

He also inherited an exceptional brain and a fine sensitive nature. His mental capacity and adult interest are a marvel to all who meet him. He has the third highest Intelligence Quotient I have given in my experience and all of his teachers report that he is the most outstanding child they have taught. His present school has been trying to interest me in sending him to a school in the East designed and run for exceptional children only, but I do not believe in this.

Not only does he have an over-all high intelligence, but he has special abilities such as writing, music, etc., and he is equally good in all subjects at school.

.... His head shaking is a nervous habit tic which comes and

*goes with stress and strain. He was particularly tired when he came
to visit you as he had just finished writing and producing his own
play, and taking a leading part in the upper school's Christmas
play. It was an honor to be chosen as the only child from the lower
school for the play and the responsibility hung heavy over him.*

Delilah's letter also introduces what can be called the "male
model" theme—the theme, that is, of Eddie's troubles stemming
from a lack of a male role model in his life. Very much the child
psychologist, Delilah explains to E.V. that the divorce "came at an
important stage in his emotional development. At approximately
six a boy transfers his interest and affections from the mother to
the father, but due to circumstances he was not able to do this.
Blocking at this important stage results in various types of behavior characteristics." Although Delilah merely hints in this letter
that E.V. might help to share the expense of sending their frail,
exceptional child to a boys' summer camp that summer "as it
would no doubt be most beneficial to him," she must have hit a
nerve because this appears to have set in motion what in later
years would become E.V.'s attempt to involve himself in Ed's
upbringing as a corrective, masculine influence.

This important letter sets the stage for the later exchanges
between Delilah and E.V. during Ed's adolescence (apparently, it
was only mutual anxiety about Ed that ever led them to have
exchanges that were at all personal), and inaugurates a long
period of uneasy concern on the part of both parents regarding
their brilliant but troubling son's development. Finally, Delilah's
letter gives us a revealing glimpse into her feelings for Eddie.
From very early on, it seems, there was a dark underside—guilt,
uneasiness, worry—to her tremendous pride in him. (Three
decades later, for instance, she would still be feeling proud yet disturbed about him—in this case regarding the gay content of his
published writing). The most striking passage in the letter has to
do with Delilah's conception of nine-year-old Eddie as someone
who possesses an extraordinary mind but is nonetheless handicapped by also having a hypersensitive nature that could spoil
what otherwise appeared to be a clear path to some sort of

renown. In characteristic fashion, Delilah's optimism overrides her fears: "I believe that he will make an adjustment in time. He will compensate through achievement, and will grow in understanding of himself and his role in life. He should make a great contribution to the world if he can maintain emotional control as he has the mental capacity for greatness."

This turned out to be wonderfully prescient, of course, but Delilah was also prescient in forecasting emotional storms that could have sunk Ed's ambitions. As later events show, it was not at all clear that Ed would survive his adolescence intact. He could very well have ended up institutionalized in a mental hospital, for example, or living near his mother, stifled and broken, an adult mama's boy.

If Eddie could be an unusually—even alarmingly—nervous and sensitive boy, he could also be "a little ham." Indeed, only a year or so after having expressed such concern about his son's well being, E.V.—who'd had his little son perform his improvised piano tinkling for guests in the years before the divorce—was showing off Eddie in the nightclubs E.V. loved to frequent across the Ohio River in Covington, Kentucky. The Beverly Hills was a particular favorite with its gambling, girlie shows, and smoky atmosphere, and once E.V. had a few drinks in him he would prod Eddie into performing a number with the house band, telling the head waiter that his son was a gifted singer. Margie, who was also on hand, remembers that Eddie would then get up on stage "in his little sport coat" and sing pop tunes. "He always seemed to rise to the occasion."

Longing for Chicago nightlife, Delilah arranged with her employer, the Illinois State Department of Special Education, to be transferred to a new area office that had opened on Chicago's north shore. She moved herself and the children back into the Georgian Hotel in Evanston in time for the 1950/51 school year. The return to Evanston meant that Eddie was once again back at his beloved Miller Elementary School (and the progressive education he thrived under) for fifth and sixth grades. These two years also constituted the height of Eddie's "weirdo" phase—the period, that is, when he became an eccentric, solitary bookworm and opera fanatic who gave no thought to his appearance or to the social impression he was making.

If from the beginning Margie had often shunned and occasionally mistreated her younger brother, she nevertheless hadn't been "embarrassed by Ed yet." But now he had become "a weird little kid. He had big horn-rimmed glasses and a crew cut and his ears were real big and they stuck out." Yet Eddie's "weirdo" phase can also be seen as one of his great intellectual periods, certainly his purest (never again, for example, would he devote more hours of the day to reading and solitary appreciation of the arts than he did in these last years before he discovered his appetite for sex and social life). "I was a loner, but I didn't even know that that was bad or unusual. And I was just tremendously fascinated by reading."

He began haunting the main branch of the Evanston Public Library, located just a few blocks from the Georgian, going there nearly every afternoon after school. Although he had no one in his life at this point to guide his reading, Eddie made continual discoveries simply by wandering through the library's open stacks on his own. One early discovery was the novels of the British author Henry Green, whose simple gerund titles caught Eddie's eye. Soon after they first came out, the eleven-year-old Eddie read *Loving, Doting,* and *Nothing.* In fifth or sixth grade his desire to read Anatole France's *Thaïs* led him to heatedly question authority for the first time. "People are always saying I'm such a wimp and have no sense of anger, but one of the ways I think I'm actually very forceful is whenever I think an injustice is being done— either to me or to someone else." In this instance he'd seen the tempting *Thaïs* in a locked case of "adult" reading material kept behind the checkout desk, but though the librarian let him handle the book for a moment—"a beautiful art nouveau edition, which had those wispy pieces of gauze paper over the illustrations and had a wonderful white binding with gold tooling"—he wasn't allowed to read it.

Convinced that "the principle of free access to books was important" and "infuriated" that *Thaïs* was off-limits to him "for some silly moralistic reason (which I didn't even grasp because Mother wasn't petty-bourgeois moralistic)," Eddie declared to the librarian, "I want to read what I want to read when I want to read it and I'm going to call the mayor." But though he did state his case to the mayor's secretary, nothing came of his protest and *Thaïs* has remained to this day a book he has not read.

Other books Eddie discovered in the stacks on his own included works on Buddhism by Christmas Humphries "who was an Englishman who had converted to Buddhism despite his name, Christmas" and Sir Edwin Arnold's *The Light of Asia*, "a versified version of the life of Buddha that featured *terrible* verse, probably the worst verse ever written." But Eddie was fascinated by the story of Buddha and though it would be a few years later that his "affinity to this curiously life-hating religion" would truly deepen, Eddie began at this time to tell others that he was a Buddhist. In fact, "one of the most embarrassing times" of Margie's youth was the night a girlfriend invited Margie and Eddie over for dinner, and "Eddie refused to eat meat because he was a vegetarian and I was just mortified." Equally mortifying was her brother's explanation for his vegetarianism—"going on and on about how he was a Buddhist."

Immersed in his "weirdo" phase as he was, Eddie nonetheless began edging out of his solitary world at this time, if only by taking a passing interest in the two eccentric and cultured adults who ran a bookstore that he had discovered in downtown Evanston: "Fred" and "Marilyn" (as the two are called in *A Boy's Own Story*, Ed can't remember their real names) were Eddie's first bohemians. A few years later Ed would discover in bohemian subculture an umbrella acceptance of all that made him weird in conventional eyes, including his homosexual predilections. He would also discover years later, running into Marilyn again, that both she and Fred were gay and had recognized all along that Ed was gay as well. When he first got to know them, however, all that Eddie was aware of—as a prepubescent fifth-grader still ignorant of his own and others' homosexuality—was that in their bookstore he'd found "everything I liked: sitting around drinking espresso coffee" (Fred and

Marilyn had an espresso machine in the store, the first Eddie had seen), "talking for hours to people about books and your feelings, and sitting on the floor in a kind of slump and reading compulsively in a bookshop. And people interested in you and thinking that you might develop into something—you were a fellow soul. Age was less important in that world. In other words, a twenty-two-year-old could talk to a twelve-year-old about books and there wasn't that feeling that you were separated by age."

Because the significance of an encounter can sometimes be all out of proportion to its duration (particularly for someone whose life, like Eddie's at this time, is relatively empty of people and incident), it comes as something of a shock for Ed to realize today that, for all the powerful impression made on him by Fred and Marilyn and the bohemian atmosphere of their bookstore, he probably went to see them only three or four times. For soon after he started visiting the bookstore Delilah banned him from ever setting foot in there again, having learned from the many nosy old ladies living at the Georgian Hotel that her impressionable young son had fallen under the influence of two "Communists" who were "living in sin." (Although, as Marilyn explains in *A Boy's Own Story*, "the truth is we're both Catholics and gay and never touched each other.") Delilah's overreaction to the situation is an early example of her anxiety over her son's "abnormal" development.

Delilah may have banned Eddie from seeing Fred and Marilyn again, but not before they had inspired him to take German lessons with a private tutor so that he could read the works of Hermann Hesse, most of whose books at that time were available only in the original German. For Fred and Marilyn, Hesse's appeal resided in his "mix of suicide, mysticism and sexual ambiguity"; moreover, although Hesse "wasn't right or even wise," the magic of reading him was "precisely as an exit out of experience and an entrance into the magic theater of sensations wholly invented." Although nothing came of Eddie's German lessons in the end (he quit before learning to speak or read the language), later on, in prep school, *Steppenwolf*—which by then he'd read in translation—became important enough to him that he would bring it up in sessions with his psychoanalyst.

꒰❀

Soon Eddie, Margie, and Delilah were living in a lakeside Evanston apartment of their own at the southern end of Sheridan Square, Delilah having at last found the courage to leave the Georgian Hotel. Here Delilah would stay put for several years. But while Delilah's and Margie's bedrooms were large and sunny, Eddie's bedroom overlooked the back alley and "was always dark and cavernous," "really a wreck," and "real smelly" from old socks and underwear. In it, Eddie would hole himself up "for hours playing those records that he got from the Evanston Library. He was serious all the time. He always seemed aloof and never quite of this world."

Nearly all the records Eddie checked out were opera. Puccini, whose "rapturous kitsch" would be the background music for much of his later adolescence, was already a favorite; there was also "a kind of delirious period where I would listen to arias being sung by Jussi Bjoerling." Other favorites included Verdi's *Requiem* and *Otello*, and Mascani's *Caviliere Rusticana*. But when Eddie sat down to listen to all of Wagner's Ring Cycle while following along with the score, he was "struck by how *slow* the music was, that the scores weren't really that thick, that one way he made the music so *long* was by playing it *slow*." This led him to dismiss Wagner as "a kind of cheat." He also disliked Mozart's operas, finding them so dull that at a Cincinnati Summer Opera production of *Don Giovanni* he felt it necessary to apologize to his companion, a newcomer to opera, whispering: "Usually it's much better than this."

When Margie's few friends would drop by the Sheridan Square apartment Eddie would sometimes emerge from his lair and start talking to them about his harp or tap dancing lessons, or what he'd been reading. Adding to the oddball impression he made was his habit of acting "very emotional about every little thing" and "always wringing his hands"—all of which would cause Margie's friends to "look at me like, 'Who is this?' Margie's humiliation in front of her friends would be compounded when

61

Delilah, rather weird herself, would come home and start "fawning over" Eddie and his achievements. "Of course he was brilliant," Margie points out, "but only his teachers and Mother would appreciate that." (In fact, it would not be until Ed was in his early twenties and living in Manhattan that Margie, after having seen a crowd lining up in the rain to purchase tickets to Ed's play *The Blue Boy in Black*, would finally feel any respect for him. In other words, she began to respect him only after having seen objective proof that others saw him as important.)

On Sheridan Square, Margie's only thought about her eleven-year-old brother was that "no one would like me" because Eddie was such a "creep." For the truth is that both Margie and Eddie were in fact perceived as "weirdos" by most people at this time, with the difference being that Margie agonized over her social status and aspired towards an ideal normality, whereas Eddie was so preoccupied with his solitary pursuits that he failed to register the depth of his unpopularity.

Yet one friend of Margie's, Penny McLeod, found neither Margie nor Eddie to be weird. Despite knowing the family since their early days at the Georgian Hotel, Penny, a sheltered minister's daughter, saw none of Delilah's despair or heavy drinking, none of Margie's smoldering resentment at feeling like a third wheel at home, and none of Eddie's kooky solitary existence. If anything, the Whites were the most fascinating characters she knew. Delilah was a warm and high-spirited woman whose "arms were wide open"; Margie was full of fun and mischief; and Eddie was a "cute" boy who was both easier and far more entertaining to talk to than her own little brother. But though Penny seems to have seen only the colorful Three Musketeers the family wanted to project and not the three losers they in fact felt themselves to be, her impressions are interesting in that they reveal that life at the Sheridan Square apartment was not entirely insulated and forlorn.

As Penny discovered, the Whites' apartment could be an enlightened, even exciting place where one could sometimes meet interesting people. One afternoon there, for instance, she met a "mixed" couple—a young white woman, who worked for Delilah, and her black boyfriend, a Northwestern University graduate student. Although interracial dating was very "far-out" behavior at the time, Penny was impressed by how modern and enthusiastic Delilah, Eddie, and Margie were about the couple. The couple eventually married.

Another witness to the Three Musketeers at this time was Delilah's former sister-in-law Helen White, who during a brief visit to Evanston was shocked by Delilah's heavy drinking (Delilah had taken the shy, sober Helen out on the town to a Chicago nightclub). On this same visit eleven-year-old Eddie had charmed his aunt by whipping up a "delicious" batch of fudge, so delicious that Helen asked him for the recipe. "I always thought he was a sweet, good-looking boy."

From Margie's point of view, however, both her mother and brother were an embarrassment. But what was even worse was when Delilah and Eddie would end up stealing all the attention—even managing to "charm and captivate" her friends— leaving Margie feeling very left out. Within the "triangle" of the Three Musketeers, of course, Margie had long felt she was in the way. Delilah would often propose that the three of them drive into Chicago for dinner at a Chinese restaurant and a Chicago Symphony concert, for instance, but Margie would almost always decline to accompany them, telling them she wasn't interested. In fact she felt unwanted and was simply feigning a lack of interest as a "defense." For Delilah had become so bound up with Eddie by this time that she was often "openly seductive" with him. For example, Margie, now a high school student, would often come home late in the evening to find "the two of them sleeping in Mother's bed together"—a state of affairs Margie found "disgusting."

Also disgusting was Delilah's habit of relying on Eddie to help her in and out of her Merry Widow, a foundation garment that was at once "a bra, a stomach flattener, a butt holder-inner" and a holder up of stockings. The Merry Widow was worn by women in the late 1940s and early 50s who wanted to approximate the Dior-inspired "New Look"—an hourglass figure with a pushed-up bust and cinched-in waist. Because the Merry Widow had so many hooks and eyes and because in any event Delilah's arms were too short to reach back and snap it all into place, she would call out to Margie to come and help her with it. But Margie, who found both the Merry Widow and Delilah's body repulsive, usually refused to have anything to do with it. "The thing that was so disgusting about it is Mother never wore underpants in her whole life. She would sit with her legs apart and her pubic hair would be bristling out underneath this girdle, the Merry Widow." (Indeed, even when Delilah was well into her eighties she was still inadvertently "flashing" people because of her lack of underwear.) Delilah would then resort to calling for her "Eddie boy," who "would go padding in there and do the Merry Widow."

Along with encouraging her son to sleep in bed with her and help her with the Merry Widow, Delilah, who was often drunk by bedtime, would also sometimes "call out from her bed and beg me to rub her back," and then "moan with pleasure" as Eddie "kneaded the cool, sweating dough" of her naked body. Though it has long been standard to conclude that a smothering, incestuous mother like Delilah must affect her son's sexuality, even "make" him gay, such a general assumption would ignore the particularities of Edmund White's life. For while Eddie's relationship with Delilah does outwardly adhere with embarrassing exactness to the classic Freudian recipe for producing a gay son, a closer inspection—as provided in the following chapter—overwhelmingly suggests that Ed was homosexual in outlook from the beginning. When looked at from this perspective it can be seen that Eddie's rubbing his drunken mother's back or sleeping in the same bed with her would have been much less sexually charged for a homosexual as opposed to a heterosexual twelve-year-old son (or, indeed, for a lesbian daughter such as Margie).

The real and quite innocent reason that Eddie involved himself in such "grotesque" and "repulsive" shenanigans with his mother is simply that it was the price of her friendship. Because he had no other friends she was the one person he could count on to give him the praise, the sense that he was needed and important and talented, that he craved. This same experience of feeling trapped and overwhelmed as the price for the gratifying sense that he was both needed and important is a pattern that has repeated itself to a lesser degree in many of Ed's close friendships with women as an adult.

❧

While Eddie never did attend the Deer Horn Boys' Camp as Delilah had proposed in her letter to E.V., he did go—in the summer of 1951—to the Culver Military Academy in Culver, Indiana. Eddie had just finishing reading a life of Napoleon and found it so enthralling that his benevolent king fantasies were now redirected into a new martial key. Eddie was also familiar with *War and Peace* and perhaps Pierre, who dreamed he might be a Napoleon and then that he might be a general who *conquered* Napoleon, had made an impression on him. This new interest in military matters led to Eddie's attempting to write a biography of Peter the Great while at the same time fantasizing that he himself would be the subject of a biography one day—after he'd become a famous general, perhaps. In fact, Eddie had the feeling that "someone somewhere" was already gathering information by recording his every move: "there was like this camera traveling around filming me. Everything I was doing had this tremendous symbolic importance"—so much so that he felt confident that "all of it would end up in the biography."

Although, at eleven, Eddie had now decided he "wanted to rule the world" and was thus excited about attending summer camp at a military academy, his actual experience at Culver—not surprisingly—proved to be a major disappointment. In fact, Eddie failed to finish his summer session at Culver, something that Delilah attributed to the fact that, like "many bright creative children, he did not like regimentation." But, ironically, what horrified Eddie even more than the Academy's regimentation was the homosexual goings-on he encountered there. Eddie was shocked to learn that his captain, a man near retirement age whose "skin was a tan mask clapped over a face that always appeared seriously exhausted," had been paying "abnormal" bedside attentions after Lights Out to Eddie's roommate "a tall, extremely shy and well bred redhead." Soon after making this horrifying discovery, Eddie fell ill with a violent fever and was sent home from camp early.

His being sent home early from Culver can also be seen as an early instance of what was to become a pattern in adolescence: his getting out of unpleasant situations by falling ill (whether psychosomatically or coincidentally). And his reaction to learning about the nature of the captain's attentions to the redheaded boy was not the only example of his prissy horror about homosexual goings-on at Culver. For when Eddie had gone into the shower room at Culver, where the boys were supervised by an adult officer, he was "shocked" that this officer turned a blind eye to "the boys all playing with each other in the shower. I thought they should be stopped."

Eddie would have been far more shocked had he known how soon and how completely his own attitude would change.

Three

Dark Currents

In retrospect Edmund White recognizes that from the beginning he "wasn't interested in little girls, I was interested in boys." His first sexual memory is of sitting on the lap of a military man as a four- or five-year-old boy. The man was a friend of the family called Jack Tommy who (the year was 1944 or '45) was visiting the White home on Beech Lane in uniform. "He was probably a pilot because as I recall he unscrewed from his lapel this little gold airplane and gave it to me. And I must have been wearing a playsuit." Ed remembers "feeling that he was attractive. It wasn't just like a physical feeling, it was an amorous feeling—that there was something warm and wonderful about him and I wanted to be with him. I must have never been touched by my father. Except spanked. But I don't think I was ever really fondled." Because E.V. was "very bristly" around other males, being held in Jack Tommy's lap was consequently "thrilling" for Eddie. (When Ed mentioned "that handsome Jack Tommy" years later to his mother, Delilah replied, "Handsome? He had big jug ears and was ridiculous looking and had bad skin." Interestingly, Ed—who would grow up to be an author accused by some critics of exhibiting a shallow "looksism" in his books—as a child hadn't yet adopted conventional notions of beauty: "Somebody who's nice to you, whose skin maybe feels warm or you like their odor, you think they're handsome.")

A passage in Ed's novel *Nocturnes for the King of Naples*, inspired by the experience of sitting in Jack Tommy's lap, portrays this encounter as stirring up the first inklings of a gay destiny.

*Placed into the heavy pages of my childhood memories are pho-
tographs ... all of men....*

*Here's one, the first in the book: a giant in khaki takes me onto
his lap and gives me a pair of gold wings from his lapel. He pierces
the frail strap of my sunsuit with the grooved pin and screws the
round, notched clasp in place. Would an ordinary boy have thanked
him then, slid off his lap and run off to play? I remain where I am.
Above me he is talking to my mother, his low voice resonating through
his body and into mine, skipping over the still water I've become ...
sinking deep into my mind, where the rings are still widening.*

While Ed does remember having a crush on one little girl in
elementary school, he concedes that it was "more friendship"
than anything else (he never imagined, for instance, what she or
other girls in class looked like naked). What's more, as a little
boy Ed once argued with another little boy about the mechanics
of heterosexual intercourse: "I told him that I was sure that men
fucked women in the ass from behind, and he said, 'No, no, they
face each other' and that women had this extra hole. I was sure
he was wrong. I knew that I was right—they did it from behind
in the ass. I remember later when I found out that in fact he was
right, I was quite chagrined."

The unfolding of Ed's sexual development now looks
inevitable, but the prospect of entering even a passing homosexual
phase would have struck the eleven-year-old Ed—who was genuinely horrified by the "abnormal" proclivities of the captain at the
Culver Military Academy—as unimaginable. It was only over the
course of the following year when he turned twelve that Ed, now a
sixth-grader, underwent a kind of inner revolution: "I went from
being very hostile to homosexuality to thinking maybe I wanted it."
The explanation for his about-face regarding homosexuality is simple: he had entered puberty and now had sexual desires.

During sixth grade Ed began wrestling with other boys, playing a game called "Squirrel" ("Grab his nuts and run") and discovering that he enjoyed the *"frottage"* offered by the game.
Although there were a number of boys he fooled around with, two
were "significant" (they're the ones whose names he remembers).

One was Cam, "a very, very pretty little boy who had very white skin, very black hair oiled and combed back in a D.A. He was tiny and he went through puberty very, very late." The other was a boy called Timmy who lived two doors down on Sheridan Square. "He was another very pretty boy, blond, with a little beauty mark on his cheek. He was rather conceited, very sure of himself. His father was a minister of the First Congregational Church. And he was somebody I would wrestle with a lot too, but not as much, not in such a sweaty, intense way as with Cam. There were other boys too like that whose names elude me." Because this kind of horse-play is rather common among twelve-year-old boys, Ed wasn't yet tormented by fears that he was homosexual.

By the following summer, when he attended a quite different summer camp—Camp Towering Pines—Ed was ready for his homosexual awakening. Yet while Ed's sexual development in real life turns out to have been a straightforward and quite logical progression, in *A Boy's Own Story* Ed deliberately made the Boy less sexually precocious because he felt that readers would find the character more appealing and universal if he were "shyer" and less "weird and perverted" than Ed himself had actually been. One effect of making the Boy less precocious, however, is to make his sexual development less logical. For while the Boy spends sixth grade hornily playing "Squirrel" with other boys just as Ed had done, the camp he attends the following summer is a Culver-like camp (which Ed had actually attended the summer after *fifth* grade). This is a crucial difference. By having the Boy go from enjoying "Squirrel" (so transparently the first real stirrings of sexuality) to being horrified by homosexual goings-on at summer camp, *A Boy's Own Story* ends up skewing the very logical consequences of puberty. For in Ed's real life the onset of puberty during sixth grade meant that from this point forward he would welcome—and actively seek out—all homosexual opportunities.

One early opportunity featured an unlikely partner: Mr. Snider, Ed's step-grandfather. During a trip to Texas to visit Delilah's parents, Ed was put in a double bed with the deformed Mr. Snider who had a wooden leg that needed to be unscrewed and taken off each night before retiring. On this particular night Ed and his step-grandfather, lying side by side in their underpants, were soon "hugging and hugging. I think he had a hard-on and I had a hard-on but I'm not even sure he did (I certainly did). He'd go 'mmm-uhmmm' and then kiss me and hug me and everything." Although the two did not actually have sex, the experience was nonetheless quite sexually charged. "He was somebody who was very deprived sexually, 'cause I don't think Grandma Snider put out at all. She was considerably older and treated him more like a sort of distinguished son. She was sort of like the peasant mother." Of course, the twelve-year-old Ed, still a virgin at this time, can also be seen as sexually "deprived"—or in any event, as so horny that he found it exciting to hug a one-legged old man all night long.

But by the time Ed wrote about the experience in *States of Desire* (1980), he had transformed his night of hugging with Mr. Snider into a sensational story of hot sex with his *grandfather* (whereas his real maternal grandfather, James Luke Teddlie, had in fact died of malaria contracted while laying railroad track through the Texas swamps when Delilah was just eleven).

My grandmother let me bunk with my grandfather and he and I made passionate, unending love all night. So far so good, but in the morning I heard him in the living room telling the others, "That Eddie is such a sweet boy, we just hugged and kissed all night long." My grandmother cooed with affection, "Well, isn't he the sweetest thang," but my mother and sister subsided into ominous silence. I slid out of bed and turned on the gas burner in the corner without lighting it; it was one of those free-standing grills, blue flames reddening bone-colored asbestos, fed by a hose out of the floor. Though I intended to kill myself I chickened out, turned off the tap and at last crept sheepishly into the living room. My mother was clearly alarmed, my sister derisive, but my grandparents beamed at me with all the charity of their innocent hearts.

The only truth in this account is that twelve-year-old Ed did indeed briefly panic and feel guilty enough to contemplate killing himself—even though, as it turns out, Margie and Delilah, far from radiating disapproval, were actually as innocent of suspicion

Ed at age two.

Christmas, 1943.

Ed with his sister Margaret.

Ed, age three, with his sister Margaret, age six.

Ed and his sister Margaret with Anna, the family housekeeper.

Above, Ed's mother Delilah, age sixteen and still living in Texas.

Ed's parents in 1924.

Ed (second from left), at Culver Military Academy, 1951.

Ed (far left), age thirteen, at his father's home in Cincinnati.

Ed, age ten, with Margaret in Evanston, Illinois.

Ed at age fourteen.

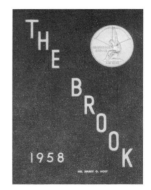

EDMUND V. WHITE

HARVARD

Entered Form IV

Ed, who is an individualist if there ever was one, is probably the most talkative boy in the senior class if not the whole school. Whenever his hand is raised in class, which happens with startling regularity, his classmates sit back to listen to another of his enormous store of fascinating anecdotes and theories. Because he can always be found spending his free time among his select group of friends discussing anything and everything no matter how large or small the subject, one might say that Ed is the intellectual leader of the Cranbrook student body. His writing talent is nothing short of fantastic as evidenced by the fact that he has already written one novel and is well on his way to completing a second. His senior year at Cranbrook found him president of the Glee Club, and holding the principal roles in the Christmas Pageant and the Operetta.

Ergasterion 4; Glee Club 5, 6 (President); Christmas Pageant 5, 6; Operetta 5, 6; Jasper Reid Award 4, 5, 6.

Ed, age eighteen, as he appeared in his 1958 prep school yearbook.

Ed at age sixteen.

Keith Fleming as a baby, with his mother Margaret
and his Uncle Ed, 1959.

Edmund White at home in Paris, 1988.

as Delilah's mother and stepfather. Nevertheless, Ed—who had never before gone so far in a homosexual experience—was so racked with guilt that he imagined his mother and sister were exchanging knowing glances. It was probably the earliest example, certainly the most dramatic expression, of the guilt and alarm he would continue to feel deep into adulthood regarding his homosexual urges.

Ed's fateful summer of 1952 at Camp Towering Pines also marks the beginning of another important theme: treachery. The summer's first betrayal, however, was committed by Delilah. Because Ed had had such a miserable time the previous summer at Culver Military Academy, Delilah decided that special inducements were needed to lure him into consenting to go to a new camp. With this in mind, Delilah tricked Ed by promising him that at Camp Towering Pines he would be "a junior counselor in charge of dramatics" (an unlikely role for a twelve-year-old boy). And yet while Ed did initially feel an infuriated sense of having been betrayed by his mother (there was no such position—indeed, no dramatics—at the camp), in the end he succeeded in mounting and starring in a ragged production of *Boris Godounov* in which he marched around in a red cape as Godounov while Tchaikovsky's opera blared from a record player. "I always wanted to be the king, of course, but then die or go crazy." He'd won permission to do Godounov "partly because I made such a big fuss" and partly because the owner of Camp Towering Pines was a friend of Delilah's. Still, it was a far cry from the many productions Ed had dreamt of staging.

Ed had driven up with the camp's owner a week before camp opened for the summer; also in tow was "a special camper"—a retarded boy that, as Ed writes in *A Boy's Own Story*, his mother

> had warned me to avoid ("Be polite, but don't let him get you alone"). She seemed reluctant to explain what the danger was, but when I pressed her she finally said, "He's oversexed. He's tried to take advantage of the younger boys." She then went on to assure me that I mustn't despise the poor boy; he was, after all, brain-damaged in some way, under medication, unable to read. If

God had gifted me with a fine mind He'd done so only that I might serve my fellow man.

In this brief parting word of warning, my mother had managed to communicate to me her own fascination with the wild boy.

Not mentioned in *A Boy's Own Story*, however, is that the special camper was in fact a *patient* of Delilah's. Delilah had long been "haunted"—in a complex, ambivalent way—by the phenomenon of homosexuality itself. Not only did she occasionally bring up the subject of homosexuality in conversation with her twelve-year-old son, but she also gave him a biography of the gay Russian dancer Nijinsky to read. For all this, now that Ed's own attitude toward homosexuality had undergone a sea change with the onset of puberty ("I was no longer such a prude and I now wanted to have sex"), it seems clear that he would have found the special camper irresistible without any prompting from his mother. Indeed, Ed wasted little time before letting the oversexed special camper, who had a constant erection that he "carried around with him wherever he went, like a scar," take advantage of him. In *A Boy's Own Story*, however, the story is told somewhat differently. The Boy and the special camper are kept apart in separate quarters and it takes weeks before the two boys find themselves alone in a climactic scene in the woods:

Where the path crossed the logger's road, Ralph [the special camper] *was sitting in a sort of natural hummock created by the exposed roots of an old elm. He had his pants down around his knees and was examining his erect penis with a disbelieving curiosity, a slightly stunned look emptying his face. He called me over and I joined him, as though to examine a curiosity of nature. He persuaded me to touch it and I did. He asked me to lick the red, sticky, unsheathed head and I hesitated. Was it dirty? I wondered. Would someone see us? Would I become ill? Would I become a queer and never, never be like other people?*

To overcome my scruples, Ralph hypnotized me. He didn't have to intone the words long to send me into a deep trance. Once I was under his spell he told me I'd obey him, and I did.

In real life Ed had sucked off the special camper almost imme-diately (and more than once). Their sex took place not out of doors but in the big cabin in which the two boys slept alone during the week before camp opened. It was the first time Ed had had sex.

Once Camp Towering Pines had opened for the summer, Ed went on an overnight canoe trip with some of the other campers. The tent that he and five other boys shared turned into a mini Sodom each night. "Two boys would play in one side of the tent, and two on the other side, and two in the middle, then we'd sort of switch around a little bit. There was lots of giggling and carrying on—I think it was actually penetration, or that's what we were trying to do." Their naughty fun was suddenly interrupted when a camp counselor burst into the tent, shining his flashlight upon them all. Ed, who was "appalled because I thought we were all going to get kicked out of the camp," was flabbergasted when it emerged that the counselor, far from wanting to turn anyone in, was in fact turned on himself and was using his flashlight to watch the boys in action. Even so, Ed (who'd failed to recognize a year earlier that Fred and Marilyn at the bookstore were gay) had no idea that this counselor was homosexual.

Ed failed to grasp this even though he'd had an earlier (and private) encounter with "Mr. Stone" (as the counselor is called in *A Boy's Own Story*) during which the counselor had shown Ed some pornographic pictures he'd taken of a nude young man on a beach, which he referred to as "art photographs."

I'd never seen a naked adult man before; I became so absorbed in the pictures that the cabin vanished and I was there before the model on that clean white sand. My eyes were drawn again and again to his tanned back and narrow, intricate, toiling hips as he ran away from me through a zone of full sunlight toward a black, stormy horizon. Where was this beach and who was this man? I wondered; as though I could find him there now, as though he were the only naked man in the world and I must find him if I were to feel again this pressure on my diaphragm, this sensation of sinking, these symptoms of shame and joy I fought to suppress lest Mr. Stone

*recoil from me in horror as it dawned on him my reactions were not
artistic. Was my fascination with the model abnormal?*

*Mr. Stone inched closer to me on the bed and asked me what I
thought of his art photographs. I could feel his breath on my shoulder and his hand on my knee. A thrill of pleasure rippled through
me. I was alarmed. I stood, walked to the screen door, made a display of casualness as I stooped to scratch a chigger bite on my ankle.
"They're neat, real neat, catch you later, Mr. Stone." I hoped he
hadn't noticed my excitement.*

The reason why he evaded the counselor's come-on is a simple one: at the time he had no idea that it *was* a come-on. For Ed's
view of homosexuality was that while boys might dabble in it as
part of passing phase it was certainly not something an otherwise
normal adult man would continue to practice. "I was excited but
I didn't think he could possibly be. I thought he was just being nice
and that they were actually artistic works. And that it was only
sick me that thought they were exciting."

The beginning of Ed's life as an active homosexual at Camp
Towering Pines is also the beginning of an accompanying shadow
theme: betraying people with whom he had sex. But though Ed
would take pride in having the courage to record in *A Boy's Own
Story* a later treachery he committed in prep school, he makes no
mention in the novel of his first betrayal, which was of the special
camper. In the book we learn only that the special camper "had
already been caught twice this summer attempting to 'hypnotize'
younger campers and was now in danger of expulsion...." In real
life Ed himself got the special camper expelled by denouncing him
to Delilah, telling her that the special camper had tried (but failed)
to seduce him as well as other innocent campers.

Why did Ed feel the need to say anything to his mother, particularly seeing as Camp Towering Pines marked the time he
stopped being a prude and began to want and have gay sex? Any
explanation must take as its starting point how "terribly confused" he was about his new homosexual desires. His having the
special camper expelled can be seen as an example of "the trap
door beside the bed"—though in this case the trap door was one

that not only hid the "evidence" that he might be homosexual from others but from his own eyes as well. Put another way: "It isn't just that I was trying to get rid of these sex partners, it was also that I felt so guilty about having sex that I wanted to pin it on them. I was trying to somehow isolate the microbe and project it onto somebody else and destroy it by destroying the other person."

And yet because ratting on the special camper only ended up arousing Delilah's suspicions that Ed himself may have been up to something abnormal, it's also possible that Ed may have been unconsciously calling attention to his "problem." Though he had "strenuously denied" that he had done anything more than repel the special camper's advances, Delilah "immediately suspected" him—asking "'Are you sure you didn't provoke this? Are you sure you didn't do anything?"

Whatever was going on inside Ed at this time, what does seem clear is that a theme had now emerged that would continue to run through his life into his adult years—the theme of his impossible desire "to be loved by men and to love them back but not to be a homosexual." And if the alternating currents of guilt and desire, "these symptoms of shame and joy," that plagued Ed were feelings shared by thousands of gay people in the 1950s, what was unusual about Ed was the extremes to which he would take and act on these commonplace feelings.

Knowing how much he had chafed under his father's yard-work regimens during summer visits, no one could have predicted that twelve-year-old Ed would *choose* to go and live with his father and stepmother for the 1952/53 school year. As it happens, Ed himself had long forgotten that it had been his own decision. Asked why he had gone to live with his father in Cincinnati, Ed thought at first that it might have been mandated by his parents' divorce agreement. Yet when this was ruled out, Ed then became fairly certain that his having told his mother about the special camper's advances must have caused his parents to agree to pack him off to Cincinnati where he could receive the benefit of E.V.'s masculine

guidance. Only when an old letter from E.V. to Delilah was redis-
covered did the truth finally come to light:

> *I am of course aware of Ed's desire to spend a year in Cincinnati. He
> talks about it a lot, when he visits. Certainly, he is welcome. I would
> enjoy having him, anytime, or as much time, as is possible. The asso-
> ciation would be pleasant, and likely, he would gain in experience
> and association. He is friendly, interested, helpful and stimulating.*

Though it will never be known for certain why Ed himself
decided to go and live with his father and stepmother, it's tempting to speculate that his decision had to do with the guilt he'd
been feeling about the disturbing sexuality that had been emerging within him throughout the past year. After all, twelve-year-
old Ed himself was already a believer in the "crackpot theory"
of the day that held that an absent father, coupled with a "sur-
feit of female company at home," could cause a boy to become
homosexual. This makes it likely that he hoped that, by joining
his father in Cincinnati, he would be able to reform himself via
the healthy influence of a "male model."*

E.V. and Kay were now living at 2300 Bedford Avenue in
Cincinnati in a large stucco house built around a patio, which stood
just a few blocks away from the old Beech Lane house. Kay had had
the house painted pink (she also had a pink Cadillac)—a daring
color scheme in the ultraconservative Cincinnati of the 1950s. But
though Margie, for one, considered the house a "horrible eyesore,"
E.V., who was fond of Mexico, found it agreeably "Spanish-y."

One of the ironies of Ed's year back in Cincinnati was that he
almost never saw his male model. There were no family evenings.
E.V., with his nocturnal schedule, would be away in the evenings
at his office in the Cincinnati Enquirer Building, asleep in the
mornings, and either still sleeping or else readying himself for
work when Ed came home from school. As for Kay, it would still
be another several years before she would feel secure enough in
her marriage to dispense with keeping an eye on her nocturnal

---

* A designation whose quite different meaning today makes Ed giggle.

husband and allow herself to "live like ordinary people"; in the meantime she continued to keep E.V.'s odd hours for the most part. More often than not Ed ate his meals alone with the maid. Further emphasizing his isolation was the remote bedroom he'd been given on the far side of the patio above the garage, a room that sat quite apart from the rest of the house. Thus by returning to Cincinnati Ed had only succeeded in coming full circle and recreating the isolation he had known as a four-year-old left at home with what E.V. referred to as the "colored help."

It was during this year that Ed's two cousins, Sue and Jean White, also came to live with Kay and E.V. for a time while their father, Bill White, was recovering from his massive stroke. Sue and Jean hardly ever saw their Uncle E.V. during their brief stay but Jean did detect an "undercurrent of friction" between Ed and E.V. The few times that Ed and E.V. were both awake and at home, Ed would be so afraid of his father that he would keep to another part of the house. Ed's relationship with his stepmother, on the other hand, was much sunnier, and they each seemed to make a real effort to get along. George Newman, the next-door neighbor boy who'd gotten to know Kay and E.V. so well, sensed that it was precisely because there was so much "tenseness between father and son" that Kay took it upon herself to act as a "buffer" between them. But Ed's cousin Jean noticed that Ed got along so well with Kay that it was almost as though he were one of her girlfriends. For Ed shared many of Kay's "feminine interests" and took pleasure in socializing with all of Kay's women friends from the Key Club, the Queen City Club, and her painting class. And when Kay, who had a naturally theatrical voice, penetrating and "dramatic," occasionally took part in amateur theatrical productions, Ed would help her out by coaching her in an English accent, for example.

Ed also organized amateur theatricals of his own at home. In much the same way as he had enlisted his two cousins in games of "King" a few years before in Dallas, he was now involving them in shows put on for the grown-ups. His cousin Sue recalls that they would all dress up for these shows and that their performances included acting out the story of Marie Antoinette. Sometimes George Newman and his younger brother joined their troupe. A photograph taken at the time shows Ed, a curled mustache painted on his face, crouched in a dramatic pose; his cousins Sue and Jean, both tall, attractive girls, are wearing long dresses, with Sue looking particularly glamorous in her satin dress and feathered hat. George Newman and his younger brother, both in costumes of their own, are also present.

If Ed had left his father's house at age seven feeling glad that the divorce had provided an escape from his father, now, five years later, he was often enough dreaming of escaping *with* him. For another irony about this year back in Cincinnati is that far from finding E.V. to be a source of wholesome masculine guidance, Ed had begun lusting after him. Feeling bored and lonely on many a morning, Ed would sit in the hall outside the louvered doors that sealed off his father and stepmother's wing of the house. As they slept on, Ed would press his ear to the louvered doors and "imagine having sex with him. Then I would imagine I could hear the sounds of them having sex, although I'm sure I didn't" (an experience that serves as a reminder of the old confusion between *lover* and *louver*). *A Boy's Own Story* provides a more passionate version of the scene:

> ... *when I was* [twelve], *I'd wanted my father to love me and take me away. I had sat night after night outside his bedroom door in the dark, crazy with fantasies of seducing him, eloping with him, covering him with kisses as we shot through space against a night field flowered with stars.*

Ed's emerging sexuality may have added a new dimension to his feelings for his father but it did not mean that he now felt any real affection for him. For while Ed would continue to feel sexually attracted to his father for a few more years, the feeling was simply lust, not love (and even this lust was more an accident of circumstance than anything personal: "I was so horny and he was the only man around.") In fact, throughout the rest of his life Ed would feel at least an initial sexual interest in practically any male he happened to be sharing living quarters with. As he writes in his short story "Watermarked": "Nothing, I suppose, is as powerful for me as the idea of actually living with someone; *living* and *sleeping* are transitive verbs for me, intimate and cherishing ones."

The male that Ed did end up seeing a lot of was another neighborhood boy whom he "introduced to Sodom and Gomorrah." But just as Ed lusted for his father but didn't like him, neither did he particularly enjoy this boy's company. In fact, Ed counts as his only friend from this period not the neighbor boy (who can be seen as Ed's first "fuck buddy"), nor George Newman and his brother, but rather another boy he knew at the Walnut Hills School, a public school for gifted children that Ed attended during this year in Cincinnati. This friend was a "big fat boy" with whom Ed worked on the school literary magazine who "played the piano marvelously well" and was a fellow social "weirdo." Of course, what Ed did enjoy about his fuck buddy—the otherwise placid and uninteresting neighbor boy—was the sex they had almost daily. Nearly every afternoon he and this boy would play the piano alone in E.V.'s house, an activity that soon made them both so aroused that they would "rush off and have sex" in Ed's secluded room. In their sex, the two boys were "just interested in getting our rocks off." That is, each boy performed the "terrible sacrifice" of getting fucked only so that he could then take his own turn. (They would tell each other, "Hurry up! C'mon, it's my turn!")

Though Ed was constantly having sex with the neighbor boy, he nonetheless felt so guilty about it that "every time after we'd finish I'd swear I'd never do it again." One day, however, a big scare occurred when Ed's stepmother walked in on the two boys. And yet the odd thing is that there was no ensuing "scandal." After the neighbor boy had been sent home, all that happened on the spot was that Ed promised his stepmother he would never do such a thing again. Kay, who was "very concerned about her own status in the world," likely chose not to reprimand the boy or tell his parents because she would have been loathe to stir up trouble in the neighborhood.

Kay had recently developed a surprisingly kinky relationship of her own with Ed. Kay had always been "very seductive, I thought, with Ed, and Ed with her," Margie recalls, but this mutual seductiveness reached strange new heights—or depths—during Ed's year back in Cincinnati. Unbeknownst to E.V., Kay had begun to give Ed "long massages with baby oil as I lay on the Formica kitchen table in my underpants"—something that led Ed to conclude that his stepmother was "quite fascinated by me sexually. I sort of felt that she was always leering at me sexually." Ed even performed "an elaborate (and very girly) striptease" for his appreciative stepmother, dancing around and stripping off clothes until he was down to his underwear: "As I became more and more feminine, she became increasingly masculine. She put one leg up and planted her foot on the chair seat, hugging her knee to her chest as a guy might. I felt I was dancing for a man."

But most bizarre of all was the enema Kay gave Ed: "Once when I told her I was constipated she had me mount the Formica table on all fours and administered a hot-water enema out of a blue rubber pear she filled and emptied three times before permitting me to go to the toilet and squirt it out."

Another interesting aspect to these kinky doings between Ed and his stepmother is that not until 1995 did Ed feel ready to write about (or more important, publish) them. But while it's true that such kinkiness would not in any event have fit into Ed's scheme for *A Boy's Own Story*, Ed nonetheless admits that he—who had so shamelessly flattered his stepmother all through his childhood and adolescence—was once again flattering Kay in his portrayal of the stepmother in both *A Boy's Own Story* and *The Beautiful Room Is Empty*, though by this time (the 1980s), with E.V. dead, it was with an eye on receiving a generous inheritance from her. When Kay did die, in 1992, Margie and Ed received much less than they'd hoped for (fifteen thousand dollars each), yet now at least Ed was free at last to write "a more realistic portrait of what a nag and bore she was." Sure enough, in the short story "Cinnamon Skin" (1995) many of Kay's more unflattering characteristics are lovingly explored:

My stepmother, Kay, was "cockeyed and harelipped," according to my mother, although the truth was she simply had a lazy eye that wandered in and out of focus and an everted upper lip that rose on one side like Judy Garland's whenever she hit a high note.

... my stepmother was short and dumpy, like my mother, though less intelligent. She'd been brought up on a farm in northern Ohio by a scrawny father in bib overalls and a pretty, calm, round-faced mother from Pennsylvania Dutch country.... Kay had done well in elocution class, and even now she could recite mindless doggerel with ringing authority—and with the sort of steely diction and hearty projection that are impossible to tune out....

Kay had spent her twenties and thirties being a shrewd, feisty office "gal" who let herself be picked up by big bored businessmen out for a few laughs and a roll in the hay with a good sport.... After Kay married my father, however, and moved up a whole lot of social rungs, she pretended to be shocked by the very jokes she used to deliver.... Her skirts became longer, her voice softer, her hair grayer, and she replaced her native sassiness with an acquired innocence. She'd always been cunning rather than intelligent, but now she appeared to become naïve as well, which in our milieu was a sign of wealth: only rich women were sheltered, only the over-protected were unworldly....

Such astute naïveté, of course, was only for public performance. At home, Kay was as crafty as ever. She speculated out loud about other people's motives and pieced together highly unflattering scenarios based on the slimmest evidence. Every act of kindness was considered secretly manipulative, any sign of generosity profoundly selfish.

An unflattering characteristic of Kay's that went unmentioned in "Cinnamon Skin" (or anywhere else in Ed's published writings), however, was her being liable, as was E.V., to fly into "terrible rages" that, still more unsettlingly, could be set off by "the craziest little things that you just couldn't predict at all."

George Newman, of whom E.V. and Kay were so fond, confirms that Kay could be riled by the most innocuous actions. Although the "chemistry" between George and Kay was nearly always "absolutely right," George had learned to be "a little careful with Kay" because she, like E.V., "had to have things her exact way." George had learned this after unintentionally infuriating

Kay once at the annual bash that E.V. threw for his employees—a lavish, catered event that constituted the only real entertaining that E.V. ever got around to doing. George's place at the table had not been allotted a cup and saucer because it was assumed that he, as a boy in his early teens, did not drink coffee. Yet when a passing waiter asked if wanted coffee, George—unaware that Kay had organized things down to the last cup and saucer needed for the affair—made the mistake of telling the waiter yes. The next thing he knew Kay had gotten wind of his request and was throwing a fit in front of everyone because an unplanned-for cup and saucer now had to be fetched. Her becoming "really upset" with him over such a petty matter was the kind of shocking experience that people remember all their lives.

Though the sparks had always flown between Margie and Kay, Margie's visit to Cincinnati during the year that Ed was living there saw things flare up so badly that Kay actually threw Margie out of the house. Margie had made the mistake of getting "snippy" with Kay, after which Kay packed Margie's bags and put her on a train back to Chicago. Ed came within a whisker of being sent back to Chicago as well when he worked up the courage to "very timidly" defend his sister—something that only succeeded in making Kay "so mad that she packed *my* bags. I had to plead with her to let me stay because I was already in the middle of the semester." That Margie "hated Kay" was apparent to both Sue and Jean White who remember that Margie, always very domineering among other girls, urged Sue and Jean to hate Kay as well.

An interesting question about Kay's relationship to Ed is whether or not she ever told E.V. about having caught Ed and the neighbor boy having sex. Ed, for his part, only knows that his father never brought up the incident (what Ed did promise his father at some point that year was that "I would never masturbate and then I did right away, of course. That was definitely the year that I was really discovering sex because I remember masturbating for hours.") Ed's guess is that E.V. must have been informed of the sodomy going on under his roof but was unable to rouse himself to take any sort of action because that "would involve actually being interested in other people."

On the face of it, this argument is not terribly convincing (particularly when one remembers that just a few years earlier E.V. had become alarmed enough about Eddie and his head-bobbing to write a long letter to Delilah). Then too, Delilah in her response had made a point of subtly reminding E.V. of his duty to provide Eddie with a male role model (something that E.V. seems to have responded to—by the time Ed was a high school student, for instance, E.V. would show again and again how seriously he took this mission). Given all this it seems likely that Kay never did tell E.V. about the incident. Margie believes that if E.V. had known about Ed and the neighbor boy's goings-on he certainly would have taken an interest (for one thing, she remembers his saying "a hundred times" that "homosexuality was worse than being a murderer"). This view also fits into what would become a pattern on Kay's part of protecting E.V. from Ed's disturbing escapades (for instance, even a quarter of a century later, in 1977, Kay fretted about the effect that Ed's coauthoring *The Joy of Gay Sex* would have on E.V.'s health).

And yet Ed today has a further, very interesting reason for believing that his father knew but didn't particularly care about his carrying on with the neighbor boy: E.V. considered sex play between two seventh-grade boys to be nothing too serious. Ed gathers his father felt this way because several years later E.V. would ask him when he'd first had sex with an adult man, as though in E.V.'s mind this alone constituted true homosexuality. E.V. had also asked Ed which parent he had been with when this occurred. Here E.V. was likely seeking to obtain "the definitive proof" that it was Delilah who was "responsible," for E.V. felt certain that it had been on Delilah's watch that the dirty deed had taken place. Instead, Ed was "triumphantly" able to tell his father that he'd first slept with an adult man during the year he'd lived in Cincinnati as a seventh grader.

This sex with an adult man occurred while Ed was on vacation with E.V. and Kay in Mexico in the spring of 1953. In these last days before jet travel, the three of them had driven by Cadillac all the way from Cincinnati, stopping over in Austin, Texas to see E.V.'s garrulous father, "Dean White," before heading down to Mexico City and then Acapulco. E.V., never particularly lavish in his Cincinnati life, would "do things very extravagantly" on the pleasure trips he would take every so often, and in Acapulco he took two rooms (one for himself and Kay, the other for Ed) at the elegant Club de Pesca. One night Ed went down to the hotel bar alone at midnight and "stood beside the piano and stared holes" into the piano player, "a jowly Indian in his late thirties," whom Ed had become "determined to seduce" after the piano player had earlier seemed to show signs of being interested in him.

Ed has twice written about what happened next, in his novel *Nocturnes for the King of Naples* and in the short story "Cinnamon Skin." The two versions, written nearly twenty years apart by a writer with no taste for rereading himself, are so consistent in their essentials that it can only mean that the experience constitutes a genuine and persistently meaningful memory, for one of Ed's methods in writing about his past is to choose only those memories that are "radioactive." When the Club de Pesca piano player took his break he led Ed, his young admirer, out of the hotel and out onto a long pier. At the far end they sat down and held hands. Just then Ed was startled to see his normally sober father drunkenly weaving his way towards them on the pier. Quickly gathering his wits about him, Ed rose to his feet and introduced his father to "Pablo," a name he made up on the spot. He then bid "Pablo" and E.V. good night and returned to his room.

Only in "Cinnamon Skin" is the evening's denouement supplied. Before being discovered on the pier by his father, thirteen-year-old Ed had managed to arrange a rendezvous with "Pablo" for still later that night in Ed's hotel room. Ed, who wrote "Cinnamon Skin" after being asked to contribute a story to *Boys Like Us: Gay Writers Tell Their Coming Out Stories*, a collection that would undoubtedly include more starry-eyed accounts of early sex, took an amused pleasure in recording this first sexual encounter with an adult man in all its brutally unromantic detail. Having found his way to the young Ed's hotel room at four in the morning,

Pablo undressed. He didn't kiss me. He pulled my underpants down, spit on his wide, stubby cock, and pushed it up my ass. He didn't hold me in his arms. My ass hurt like hell. I wondered if I'd get blood or

shit on the sheets. He was lying on top of me, pushing my face and chest into the mattress. He plunged in and out. It felt like I was going to shit and I hoped I would be able to hold it in. I was afraid I'd smell and repulse him. He smelled of old sweat. His fat belly felt cold as it pressed against my back. He breathed a bit harder, then abruptly stopped his movements. He pulled out and stood up. He must have ejaculated. It was in me now. He headed for the bathroom, switched on the harsh light, washed his penis in the bowl, and dried it off with one of the two small white towels that the maid brought every day. He had to stand on tiptoe to wash his cock properly in the bowl.

When Ed informed his father a few years later that his first sex with a grown man had been with the Club de Pesca's piano player, E.V. countered by telling Ed that on a subsequent trip to Acapulco he'd heard that Pablo "had been caught molesting two young boys in the hotel and had been shot dead by the kids' father, a rich Mexican from Mexico City." Ed was never able to find out whether this had indeed happened or whether it was "just a cautionary tale dreamed up by Daddy. Not that he ever had much imagination."

Another trip Ed took with his father and stepmother that year was to New York City. En route to New York on the new interstate highway, they were waylaid by a freak blizzard and forced to stay over at an overflowing motel where they made do sleeping on billiard tables and lobby sofas because all the beds were taken. Once they'd made it to New York, however, things were every bit as glamorous as they'd been in Acapulco. They checked into E.V.'s favorite hotel, the Roosevelt, and dined at his favorite restaurant, Asti's, an establishment in Greenwich Village catering to opera buffs where both customers and waiters got up and sang arias to piano accompaniment. Ed, who even as a small boy had had the pluck to run backstage to get the autograph of the conductor Sir Eugene Goosens, walked over to a neighboring table at Asti's that night and with "kamikaze bravado" introduced himself to Jerome Hines, "the Metropolitan *basso,* who graciously invited us to sit in his box the next night and hear him sing the role of the high priest in *The Magic*

Flute. What impressed me the most was the scene where the lovers pass through fire and water; the illusionism of the water, a great cataract plunging from the top of the stage, was uncanny, inexplicable, though I found the music itself a disappointment...."

This performance of *The Magic Flute* took place at the old Metropolitan Opera House, "which was down in the forties on Broadway, a beautiful old house." The spectacular special effects made it one of the most dazzling moments of Ed's youth.

Ed remains as hazy about why he decided to leave his father and return to Evanston and Delilah for the 1953/54 school year as he is about why he chose to spend this "lonely, lost year" under his father's roof in the first place. While it might be tempting to suppose that Ed yearned to be reunited with his mother, still his biggest and in fact only real supporter, the truth is that Ed didn't miss her all that much during this year away from her. This tallies with his decision to go to Cincinnati in the first place as well as with a consistent habit of mind running throughout his entire life: for Ed, all people absent, including his mother, are very much out of sight, out of mind. "When I was with Mother I would be fascinated by her and kind of hypnotized by her, but when I was away from her I don't remember being homesick."

Perhaps his returning to Evanston was as simple as his having decided that one year with his male model had been quite enough and that it would simply remain to be seen whether the hoped-for corrective influence had done its work. Alternatively (and more likely, given that Ed rarely saw his male model and in any event continued to develop homosexually while in Cincinnati), Ed may have decided that because no good had come from living with his father there was no point to staying on.

One of the most intriguing turning points in Ed's life occurred back in Evanston when, as an eighth-grader at Evanston's Haven Junior High, he "changed overnight," as his sister observed, into a "socialite." This turning point is all the more intriguing because

Ed's gregariousness is something that has become so much a part of him—it's one of his defining characteristics from this point on—that it now seems mysterious that something so fundamental to his nature didn't surface until age thirteen or fourteen. One possible explanation is that until this point he'd moved so often from school to school that he'd never had the chance to get to know his classmates very well. Haven Junior High (although Ed, as a resident of south Evanston, was supposed to attend Nichols Junior High, Delilah had "finagled it" so that he could attend the academically superior Haven in wealthier north Evanston) was in fact his sixth school in eight years. But while this explanation might account for his relative lack of friends before eighth grade, it does not explain why he suddenly became so sociable at Haven, which after all was yet another school with another new set of kids for him to adjust to.

Another possible explanation for his late-blooming sociability is that up till now he had modeled his behavior on that of his "weird and isolated" parents. Neither Delilah (who spent most of her time with those she called "the Little People"—her mentally retarded charity patients and their parents) nor E.V. (who knew only clients and the people who worked for him) took part in the local community or had much of an idea how to cultivate real friends. On the other hand, this notion fails to take into account that many of Ed's interests—his interests in kings, books, and bohemianism, for example—had no basis whatever in his parents' behavior.

In any event, the year in Cincinnati is when his interest in social life finally awakened, for it was only there, away from his mother, that it occurred to him that he didn't have any friends. Now that he had returned to Evanston for eighth grade and was living with Delilah once again, he realized that the best escape from loneliness—as well as from her—was through a circle of friends.

Whatever new attitude toward friendship Ed may have formed by eighth grade, the key event in his becoming more socially connected occurred about halfway through the school year when he read aloud one of his poems to the kids in various homerooms throughout Haven Junior High. This unexpected, even unprecedented reading tour had come about when one of Ed's teachers, a Mrs. Kincaid, invited him to read a long poem in rhymed couplets that he'd written for a class assignment. While Mrs. Kincaid had found Ed's poem to be impressive, she was careful not to overpraise it, declaring that the poem revealed "A small spark that will some day break into flame, perhaps." But it was precisely because she was so qualified in her praise that Ed found it more gratifying than Delilah's praise, which was always "over the top." Still more surprising was the reaction of some of the kids to his poem: "It was just a freaky thing but they all thought it was neat and I became very friendly with a bunch of kids." One new friend was Butch Dastic, a "very handsome, sexy, young Marlon Brando type." Two other new friends were Howie and Buster, "both very sweet and sexy. They were football players—big, stocky boys—but they were very intellectual, maybe because they were from intellectual Jewish families. So it's sort of funny that literature brought me friends from the very beginning."

Rounding out Ed's new friends was Butch Dastic's girlfriend, Sue Hemb. It was in the basement of Sue's house that Ed discovered the world of after school get-togethers, "where you'd close the curtains and you'd all be slow dancing to Brenda Lee's 'Break It to Me Gently.' It was all to do in a way with sex and of course I was very in love with Butch Dastic who I thought was just divine." Around Butch and Sue in particular Ed adopted the role of a "kind of court jester" who—as Ed played the role—was more adept at flattering than amusing people, an emphasis well-suited to Ed's personality skills, "which really were molded on endlessly flattering and pleasing my mother."

Because Ed had been so intensely involved in his life of going to the library every afternoon and listening to opera in his room, he hadn't realized that some of his classmates often saw one another socially outside the classroom. But now that he was friends with Butch and Sue, Buster, and Howie (who also began to invite Ed home after school), this led to a few more friendships. Thus in the space of a few short months Ed went from being "a total loner to having six or seven friends," and though he was still more of a "hanger-on" than someone truly popular, these six or seven new friends were nonetheless the start of Ed's transformation into the social dynamo he has been ever since.

This emergence as a social being was so important for Ed that only now did he feel he'd truly become a person. If it had taken the disruptions and new order brought about by his parents' divorce to make him aware that he had a life, it took having friends to convince him he'd become "a character, perhaps even a person, since if to be is to be perceived, then to be perceived by many eyes and with envy, interest, respect or affection is to exist more densely...." Before his "great conversion" into a person, Ed had given no thought to how he looked. This disregard for his personal appearance was due to his being both uninterested as well as uninformed—uninterested, because he had seen no point to grooming himself in his solitary world; uninformed, because Delilah had never bothered to teach him how to clean or dress himself and rarely bought him clothes. In fact, before the divorce Anna the maid had exclaimed to Delilah one day, "This poor little boy's in rags!"

Now that he had friends and cared about how he looked, he allowed his sister Margie to teach him how to roll up the cuffs on his few pairs of blue jeans (Ed had been wearing them, as Margie recalls, "dragging down in the dirt and they'd get all frayed and everything"), and to get him a pair of tennis shoes to replace his "nerdy" black Oxfords (which Margie had dismissed as "old boat shoes"). His sister also

> *knew precisely what would appeal to my classmates ... which red-and-white-checked short-sleeved shirt.... ("You've got to roll up the sleeves exactly three times—the folds should be tight, see?—and no more than an inch wide"). She taught me to say hi to as many people as possible in the school corridors, to notice with care who responded and to brave each blank stare with a glittery smile.*

Although *A Boy's Own Story* portrays the Boy's new friends in eighth grade as having freed him from his mother ("As long as I remained unpopular I belonged wholly to my mother"), in reality Ed had been drawing away from Delilah since the previous fall when he'd elected to spend the year in Cincinnati with his father. It can even be argued that since the arrival of puberty in sixth grade Ed had become increasingly involved with his emerging homosexuality (both its desires and the guilt this inspired) and no longer had time for all the old intensities of his relationship with Delilah. It's also very possible that he was now intellectually outgrowing her as a friend, as he would come to outgrow other adult friends. Then too, Ed's year away from Delilah must have given him some perspective on just how consuming his relationship with her had been since the divorce—a relationship that had been as demanding as "a love affair with a difficult, neurotic, and unstable person."

Though Ed had begun his move toward greater independence from his mother before this year in eighth grade, now that he had friends of his own his drawing away from her began to accelerate—something that Delilah reacted to by becoming possessive as well as "very seductive" with him. For while Ed remained preoccupied with male friends such as Butch, Buster, and Howie whom he idolized and secretly lusted after, he had also come to know a handful of girls that he would see occasionally. He'd come home from having been out with a gang of kids, including some girls, and find that his mother "would be drunk and in bed and want me to rub her shoulders. She was always, I felt, very kind of jealous that I would go out with other girls." Early on in his new-found popularity at Haven, for instance, he was invited by a girl to attend a sock hop at the Evanston YMCA and Delilah had been terribly upset about it.

There was more to Delilah's behavior than simple possessiveness, however. Much of her intrusiveness can be attributed to her simply being unaware of how modern, middle-class moms conducted themselves. Delilah, after all, was someone who had known only rural, lower-middle-class family life while growing up in Texas. Even now in middle age she had managed to remain largely ignorant of middle-class family conventions by being so preoccupied with her professional life and night life that she never participated in Evanston social life and thus never experienced any social pressure from fellow parents to conform to local norms. As a teenager on a Texas farm she'd always been very bound up with her family and thus had no idea, for instance, that modern adolescents preferred to draw away from their parents as they got caught up in the world of their peers. Then too, she seemed not to know how "weird" and "invasive" it was to be coming into Ed's room without knocking, or to be regularly asking him how he was developing physically. Ed remembers that even after he'd become a young adult he'd had to tell a friend of the family, "Oh, my mother is sobbing and creating a big scene because I won't spend New Year's Eve with her," only to learn (since Ed himself was still ignorant about how most families handled holidays) that "*Christmas* is for family, dear, New Year's is for your date."

But as much as Ed resented his mother's intrusions, there remained within him what had long been two strong and contrary currents of feeling for her. "It was a very symbiotic relationship in which there was one part of me that was very passive and wanted to be totally absorbed by her, and there was another part of me that was rebellious and wanted to escape her. I think the part that loved life and wanted to grow was the part that wanted to escape her. In other words, you could think of it as Eros and Thanatos. The Thanatos part wanted to be merged with her and the Eros part wanted to escape her."

What remains somewhat mysterious about Ed's transformation into a social being—into a "person"—is why it took him so long. One scenario would be that he had always hungered for the friendship of other kids, as Delilah's story about his tears in Texas when a classmate showed his knife to everyone but him would seem to show. In this view Ed's unusual and precocious personality, which was always better appreciated by adults, together with his changing schools so often, kept him effectively friendless until eighth grade when he was at last accepted by some especially "neat" kids who were impressed by his poem. A more convincing argument, however, is that before puberty Ed had had little interest in other kids. Delilah had long been fond of saying that "It's not that the other children don't like Eddie, it's that Eddie's not interested in the other children."

In this view, Ed—who had grown accustomed to being displayed as a prodigy by his mother to her friends—had been happy enough to exist on a purely artistic and intellectual plane where the few people he was drawn to were adults (such as Fred and Marilyn at the bookstore) who shared his interests. Once his sexuality came into play, however, he not only began to take an interest in kids his age but now had something in common with them, something he could *do* with them (whether it was playing "Squirrel" or fooling around with other campers at Camp Towering Pines). In other words, only by becoming sexual did Ed become sociable—the sexual, that is, preceded and made him interested in the social. Seen this way what then becomes interesting about his friendships with the kids at Haven—Butch, Buster, and Howie—is that here all the elements of Ed's personality were at last brought into play: they on their side admired Ed for his writing talent, while he on his side found them sexy (indeed, it could be argued that many of Ed's relationships throughout the rest of his life have had their foundation in precisely these terms).

Another development in Ed's life at this time that was deemed too sexually precocious for inclusion in *A Boy's Own Story* was his friendship with "Tex" (Ed doesn't remember his real name), a "small Texan with bad eyes, bad skin, and the smell of Luckies on his breath" who owned a book and record store near Chicago's Loop.* On afternoons when Ed was not getting together with his new friends after school, he had begun riding the El into Chicago to spend a hurried hour or so in Tex's "cozy store," located on Rush Street, with an art film cinema on one side and an espresso shop on the other, before rushing back home for dinner. Tex and his "pouty assistant Morris" were reminiscent of Fred and Marilyn and their bookstore, with the difference that Tex and Morris were openly gay and Ed now old enough for Tex to serve as a kind of gay mentor.

Through his visits to Tex's store, Ed quickly discovered the existence of a "gay world."

> *The bitter coffee we drank, the sound of the discreetly murmuring announcer on the classical music radio station, and the sight of reflected spotlights tilting off varnished new books and records*

---

* Ed's encounters with "Tex" are portrayed in the sequel to *A Boy's Own Story*, *The Beautiful Room Is Empty*, in which the Boy is nearly eighteen when these encounters take place, not thirteen or fourteen as Ed was in real life.

still in their cellophane wrappers—all of these things came together to excite me, especially since I knew Tex was gay....

Ticking steadily inside me was the thought, half-thrill half-fear, that within my grasp, or almost, lay this other world. This "gay world," you might say.... Although I knew something would have to come out of my visits if I continued paying them, I feared what I hoped, and what I hoped I didn't want to know.

What did end up coming of Ed's visits was that Tex, who "was so intimate that he erased the distance between adolescent and adult," taught the thirteen-year-old Ed some fundamental facts and notions of gay life, including the fact that a blow job does not entail any actual blowing. Ed also ended up having sex once with Tex in Tex's dingy hotel room:

... he kissed me and massaged my shoulders and back with surprisingly strong hands, then he explained step by step what we were about to do. Always the good student, I responded competently, never guessing I was meant to feel any pleasure.

The minute I came, a wave of sickening guilt rushed over me. The hotel room looked depressing. I noticed the stain on Tex's underpants and the hole in his stocking. Down the hall someone was coughing....

I pecked him on the cheek, barely able to conceal my shame and disapproval. He yawned. I hurried down the cold street, my mouth sour from Tex's cigarettes, my cock and ass glowing, my heart sinking, sunk. I swore to myself I'd never, never sleep with another man.

Despite his promises to himself, this 1953/54 school year marked the beginning of Ed's cruising for sex. While Ed had progressed socially from an interest in eccentric adults to kids his own age, sexually he had progressed from kids to anonymous sex with adult men. Though it seems to have been sex that awakened Ed to a real interest in kids his own age, in the realm of sex Ed soon came to the realization that he himself was more interesting to grown men than to other kids: "Whereas I felt like a nerd with other kids my own age, I recognized that on the open market of pedophiles I did have a high value. The truth is there were so few boys as crazy and forward as I was whom a pedophile could pick up on a beach or in a toilet or whatever and have sex with. In other words, they have to usually spend months and months coaxing somebody—especially a kind of nice suburban boy like me. I never saw anybody my own age when I would go cruising. Very few teenaged boys in the 1950s had sex, and if they did, they had it with each other and they didn't go out looking for adults."*

One afternoon when he was twelve or thirteen Ed was watching a movie in a theater in downtown Cincinnati when a man suddenly joined him and "put his raincoat over our laps and fondled me. And I loved that." Because he was nearly full-grown already, he was often mistaken for being several years older, particularly in the dark. By the following year, as an eighth-grader at Haven, Ed had begun regularly cruising men himself. How did such a bookish boy get the idea to cruise? "In my case it was the library. People would write graffiti on the walls and say, 'If you want a blow job, come here' and then I would come there. Somebody would put down a precise hour and a date, and I'd be there and then they wouldn't be, of course." Thus the world of literature can be said to have won Ed his first real friends as well as introduced him to the world of cruising.

From the start Ed never felt so apprehensive while cruising that he would suddenly back out. "I must have been kind of tingly and excited and scared, but I was so driven." His earliest cruising was done at the men's room of the Howard Street Elevated Station. Howard Street, with its seedy liquor stores, marked the border between Evanston (which was dry) and Chicago, and the Howard Street Station was within walking distance of the Sheridan Square apartment. Soon Ed had mastered the mechanics of men's-room cruising. For example, he learned that the reason few heterosexual men ever encounter a men's-room come-on is that "straight people look for the maximum space," while gays "wait for a reciprocal signal. Let's say there were five urinals and

---

* This early cruising was also something that Ed felt was too bold and sexually precocious for *A Boy's Own Story*.

a man might be on the one at the extreme right. If you chose the one on the extreme left you'd be straight, but if you chose the one in the middle you'd be gay. Then you sort of stand there and if you don't hear any tinkling of water, you realize the person's just standing there and then you start stealing glances at each other."

Ed was unconcerned about the looks of the men he began to pick up—middle-aged married men, for the most part—because he was in "such a fever." And while he himself felt no fear, the men who picked him up certainly did. "You have to remember people are so terrified of anybody young because they could go to jail for it, so if you were a sex maniac child like me it was very hard to get anybody to ever have sex with you. And if they did, you could never see them a second time." Because it was too risky to do anything beyond some *"touche pipi"* in the men's room, Ed would climb into the cars of the men he picked up. If the night was warm, they would drive to the lakeside to have sex; if cold, to a deserted lot for sex in the car.

While admitting that most gay people today would never think in such terms, Ed is convinced that his early homosexual cruising was, secretly, a "form of sexual rebellion" against his mother. "I'm not saying what's a cause and what's an effect—all I know is that whenever I would feel too oppressed by my mother I would long to get away and to be in this all-male world of sexuality. And if I could go off and suck somebody off at Howard Street Station I would feel like a cat that had swallowed the mouse."

One sign of how much his early cruising had to do with secret rebellion is what an unusually small role direct physical pleasure played in the sex he had: most of the time Ed "would suck people off and wouldn't even masturbate myself." All through adolescence, in fact, his own penis would play little or no part in his promiscuous sex life—a phenomenon that can be seen as part of Ed's need to court everyone, including anonymous sex partners, as well as—later—a desire to have sex with the most attractive men possible (men who might consent to be "serviced," that is, but nothing more). But perhaps a better answer to the riddle of Ed's having been a "sex maniac" whose own penis was almost never involved is that it assuaged his guilt about his homosexuality somewhat. For as he confides in his second autobiographical novel, *The Beautiful Room Is Empty*: "I had no desire (no *vulgar* desire I might have said) to obtain sexual release. In my eyes, my preference for service to others over personal pleasure mitigated my corrupt desires."

It also seems fairer to say that his secret rebellion was directed not so much personally against his mother as against all authority figures in his life. For Ed was often smoldering with hidden resentment about having "to obey my parents, my teachers, and conform to society. And every once in a while, as an expression of personal freedom and of my anger and the principle of anarchy and individualism that was so ardent within me, I needed to do something that was antisocial or that they would be appalled by. But I was also such a goody-goody that I didn't want something that would become known."

Interestingly, this same impulse to be "a monster child without anybody knowing" can be found in much earlier, unsexual episodes in his life. As a boy of seven, for example, Ed had taken to stealing stale cigarettes that his father kept on hand for guests and smoking but not inhaling them in the basement of a decrepit recreation center that E.V. had enrolled him and Margie in during the first summer after the divorce. And at the Faust Hotel in Rockford, Illinois, Ed had mildly tortured a pet hamster by placing its feet on a "horribly hot metal lamp shade." What all these acts had in common was that they brought him no pleasure, only the satisfaction of knowing that "if there was a camera filming me all the time—and I oftentimes thought there was in my paranoid delusions of grandeur—the camera would be able to see that I really was my own man and very wild." In this view forbidden cigarettes, animal torture, and homosexual sex all gave Ed, an otherwise dutiful and even over-accommodating boy, the feeling that "I wasn't completely under their thumb— or it was like a way of getting back at them."

During this watershed year in which Ed awoke to both social life and cruising, he was also becoming deeply interested in Buddhism. As with his other new interests, his interest in

Buddhism has a sexual explanation—"a gay scenario." For as someone who had just started cruising and felt tormented about yet driven to satisfy his hunger for gay sex, Ed found the ascetic side of Buddhism—its focus on eliminating desire—appealing. Although he had been interested in the East for several years already, it was only during this year that he began reading about eastern religions in earnest after discovering that he could slip into a library on the Northwestern University campus. Perhaps because he looked so much older than thirteen, he was taken for a college student. Wandering through the open stacks he discovered Max Muller's *Sacred Books from the East*, "a whole library of books that he'd translated: the Upanishads, the Bhagavad Gita, all that, but also a lot of the Buddhist sutras." *

As he read through *Sacred Books of the East* he considered various religions "as one might try on clothes—but isn't Hinduism just a bit busy? Confucianism? Too sensible, no flair." Of the two main branches of Buddhism—Hinayana and Mahayana—Ed was drawn to the older Hinayana because it was "more rigorous and more monastic" as well as atheistic. Mahayana Buddhism, in which followers are obliged to postpone their own nirvanas in order to save everyone else, "sounded too much like Christianity and saints and everything to me. Hinayana was all about being alone and being a monk." Hinayana Buddhism was thus very much in keeping with Ed's deep-seated feeling that he "owed nothing to anyone," which was after all the flip side of the early loss of faith in people he continued to feel after the "double betrayal" of the belt whipping.

Ed's first major friendship had its origins in a quite cynical calculation on his part. Wanting to increase his popularity during freshman year at Evanston High School, he decided to cultivate the friendship of the most popular boy in the freshman class, Steve

---

* J.D. Salinger's characters Seymour and Buddy Glass owned as teenagers the complete set of Muller's *Sacred Books of the East* (like Ed, Seymour had discovered Muller on his own). Yet at this time (1953/54) Ed couldn't have known about the Glass brothers since "Zooey" wasn't published in *The New Yorker* until 1957.

Turner, calculating "that if I could hoodwink him into being my friend, people would have to accept me." Ed also calculated that all a marginal and unathletic boy like himself could offer such a natural prince who was captain of the school tennis team was "the flattering mirror of my attention, a service that suited my sweet, devious nature." But what made it possible for Ed even to approach Steve Turner was Steve's own conscious willingness to mix with a wide spectrum of kids, from "hoods" to "a number of friends who weren't very macho." It was this same refusal to be "cliquish" or to be guided by stock, superficial judgments about people that Steve feels explains his enormous popularity at Evanston High. And so while his first impression of Ed was of a "nerdy" and "sissy" boy standing on the sidelines in gym class watching the other boys play kickball, Steve didn't hold it against him.

Yet his openness to someone as different as Ed nearly got him into a fight. Soon after he and Ed had become friends, Steve had a "dramatic" confrontation with "a group of toughs" who warned him there were rumors circulating that Ed was queer. These toughs included Butch Dastic, the boy that Ed had found so "divine" the previous year at Haven Junior High. Refusing to believe such a terrible thing could be true about his new friend, Steve angrily defended Ed, almost coming to blows with some of the boys. Nonetheless, the incident sat uneasily with him because he knew how rare it was at relatively liberal Evanston High to label someone queer and that it was never done idly. Sure enough, a week or so later came the news, impossible to deny, that Ed "had made advances" to some boys in the freshman class.

The news filled Steve with a mixture of "anger and disappointment," but he decided to make it a point of honor not to break things off with Ed, enduring the scorn of some of his classmates. He also never told Ed about nearly getting into a fight with Butch Dastic and the other boys or about the shocking confirmation of their charges. All that he did say—on the first of many nights that Ed slept over at his house—was that any homosexual "weird stuff" would not be tolerated and would in fact end their friendship. This accomplished, Steve never felt anything less than "comfortable" around Ed and to his surprise the two of them went on to have "a very warm and in many ways tender friendship," keeping in touch with each other even after Ed had gone off to prep school and college, and seeing each other summers.

Steve had thought at first that Ed's sexuality would limit their friendship because "the fact that he was gay shut him out of some of the possibilities—we couldn't interact in the same way," but the irony is that Ed's homosexuality is in fact what made the friendship flourish. For though Ed's original attraction to Steve had been to use him as a means of increasing his popularity, now that they were friends Ed had quickly fallen head over heels in love, a love he found "all the more powerful because I had to hide it." And because he felt forced to keep his love a secret, Ed threw his energies into becoming the best friend that Steve had ever known, lavishing on him the kind of artful attention that only an experienced courtier can provide.

Despite his wide-ranging contact with all kinds of kids, Steve had never before been listened to and encouraged by someone with such wily knowledge of how to flatter the male ego. Ed would amplify Steve's enjoyment of his own mind, for example, by skillfully fleshing out Steve's halting ideas as though he were merely suggesting what Steve had meant to say. Then too, it became "almost automatic" for Ed to defer to Steve in everything. Ed never spoke of his interest in opera, for instance, because "it would have gone through two or three filters before it got to that. I would have thought, I wonder if I said that would he think I'm weird? Is he interested? Oh, he's interested in folk music, I'll be interested in folk music."

Although Steve had originally felt that Ed's being gay meant they wouldn't be able to talk about girls, such a big part of heterosexual male conversation, he soon found himself talking about everything with Ed—including girls—in a way he never had with other boys. During the many nights Ed slept over at Steve's house, the two boys "sat around for hours in our underpants and talked about Sartre and tennis ... and all the other kids at school and love and God and the afterlife and infinity." "I loved to be with him because he was a *very* entertaining person," Steve remembers. When they'd go to a party together, for instance, they'd talk about it afterwards and "it was like he'd been to a totally different event than I had. He had a way of seeing things and hearing things and arranging thoughts that was very dazzling. I love to hear Eddie tell stories—the best storyteller I ever knew."

But though what underlay the whole friendship was Ed's feeling "so interested in seducing him that I was always trying to please him as a friend," Steve, oddly enough, never had a clue that Ed was in love with him. Having drawn the line early on about not tolerating any funny stuff, he regarded the entire subject as closed—as though Ed's unfortunate homosexual tendencies were something strictly sexual and general in nature and didn't include the possibility of love, especially a love of him in particular. Steve remained so completely unaware of Ed's love that, decades later when *A Boy's Own Story* was published, he was shocked to read how Ed had really felt about him: "Now I know what it's like to be a sex object."

The two teenage friends who talked about everything would also sometimes discuss how Ed's homosexuality might be "overcome" (thus putting Ed in the paradoxical position of telling the boy he loved how desperately he wanted to be cured). Over the next few years Steve would always be aware of the "awful struggle" Ed was going through in trying to subdue his persistent homosexuality: "One of the things that I kept thinking was that somehow, given the right stimulus and situation, he would learn to be a real man." With this in mind Steve came up with several plans of action over the years, including taking Ed on a camping trip in the Quetico lake country* and, later, finding Ed a summer job driving a truck. "If somehow he could see the light or get some help, he could change that pattern or that predisposition, and somehow this would help him get over that problem. And I thought of it as a problem."

But Steve's first and most significant plan of action was taken in the spring of their freshman year at Evanston High when he arranged for Ed to go on a date with a girl. This date, which was to be a key event in Ed's adolescence with important consequences,

* This camping trip, on which Ed and Steve Turner were joined by their mutual friend Dan Passoja, is the subject of Ed's short story "Pyrography."

came about when Steve invited Ed along on a double date one evening. Ed's date was to be a girl named Sally, a voluptuous brunette who was "famous for the great globes of her breasts, as evident as her smile and almost as easy to acknowledge," but who had lately acquired a snooty reputation for considering herself to be too "mature" for her fellow freshmen. Many of her dates, in fact, were with college boys. "She looked down her nose a bit at typical high school shenanigans," Steve Turner remembers. "She was a little bossy."

Such a thrilling opportunity had opened up only because Sally's current boyfriend happened to be laid up at home with the flu. Though the date consisted of nothing more than a movie at Evanston's Coronet Theatre, followed by a bite to eat and walking Sally home, it was enough to make Ed believe he had fallen madly in love with her. More astoundingly, by the time their short date had ended, Ed had convinced himself that Sally was his ticket to a healthy heterosexual life and that the new and uplifting love he felt for her meant that "An oppression had been lifted. A long apprenticeship to danger had abruptly ended. At last the homosexual phase of my adolescence had drawn to a close."

Ed decided to write Sally a declaration of love on parchment paper. He even consulted a book on italic lettering in an effort to improve his miserable handwriting (an effort that failed; Ed's handwriting has remained so unreadably bad that all his adult life he has dictated his written drafts to a typist). Along with his declaration of love, Ed included a "pornographic" sonnet he had composed especially for Sally with lines like "Let me lick your bosom." A week or so later Sally's polite rejection arrived in the mail. Ed's devastation over this loss marks the beginning of an important transitional period during which he went from being immersed in his life at Evanston High to wanting to go off to boarding school. For now that Sally had crushed his hopes of becoming heterosexual, he became convinced in his despair that he had been condemned to a horrible "homosexual fate." A year and a half later, at age sixteen, he would begin work on his first novel, the autobiographical *Dark Currents*, in which the hero's sexuality hangs precariously in the balance before being "tipped" into homosexuality by a girl's rejection.

Although in *A Boy's Own Story* the Boy's attraction to the Sally character ("Helen Paper") is explained by her prominent social status, so that the Boy's interest in her neatly parallels his friendship with the Steve Turner character ("Tommy Wellington") in that he hopes the girl's popularity can be conferred on him if he becomes her boyfriend, in real life Sally was not popular at Evanston High. Steve Turner, in fact, has always wondered why Ed chose to make Sally such an important figure. But the explanation is quite simple: Sally happened to be the one girl with whom Ed had a date during this time when he felt a girl's love could redirect his sexuality.

It's easy to see now that Ed's hope of going straight through the love of a girl was as doomed as his chances of making Sally fall in love with him. Though there were many girls who were fond of Ed, and though it was invariably female classmates and teachers who found him "special," Steve Turner was aware that the girls at Evanston High "didn't find him romantically attractive" because they intuitively seemed to sense he was gay. Thus by setting things up in his mind so that everything hinged on a girl almost certain to reject him, Ed would seem on some level to have been seeking to exonerate himself from responsibility for being gay by dramatizing the idea that he had been driven into it.

Doomed as he now felt to a homosexual fate, Ed was nonetheless unprepared to be pointed out as gay in public. Shortly after being rejected by Sally in the spring of 1955, Ed spent an evening with Morris, the assistant to Ed's gay mentor Tex, on Chicago's North Side. Morris had brought along some campy gay friends and the evening became Ed's first gay night on the town. If Tex had introduced Ed to technique, Morris and his friends now introduced him to camp style. For the first time Ed heard one "queen" say of another, "She covers the waterfront, poor dentureless crone, looking for seafood trade," for instance, or call out to a passing policeman, "Love your hat, Tilly!" The evening ended up having all the effect of a gay "outing" for Ed when Morris and his friends continued their carrying on in a coffee shop and the stares of surrounding straight people made Ed realize with horror that "For the first time I'd crossed the line. I was no longer a visitor to the zoo, but one of the animals."*

Ed may have crossed the line but it would be another six months or so before his parents were made dramatically aware of this. For the time being Delilah and E.V. still had no inkling that their son was now living out the idea that he was doomed to a homosexual fate. Ed's long visit to E.V.'s Walloon Lake summer house in northern Michigan that summer turned out to be the last time he spent with his father that was unclouded by the issue of homosexuality. The opening chapter of *A Boy's Own Story* is a portrayal of this summer of 1955; that this first chapter is also an elegy to E.V. can be seen in the substantial and somewhat idealized portrait of his father that Ed composed. For it was E.V.'s death in early 1979 that both inspired and freed Ed to begin writing the novel in the first place (so long as E.V. remained alive, Ed felt "afraid to write about him. Fear had always been my main response to him").

When Ed began work on *A Boy's Own Story* the first thing he wrote about was the one interest that he and his father had ever shared: listening to E.V.'s records (mostly the works of Brahms, Mahler, and Wagner)—"the recorded concert that filled the house deep into the night, even until dawn." Ed's description of their mutual interest in music is probably the most striking passage in the entire novel:

> *I never showered with my dad, I never saw him naked, not once, but we did immerse ourselves, side by side, in those passionate streams every night. As he worked at his desk and I sat on his couch, reading or daydreaming, we bathed in music. Did he feel the same things I felt? Perhaps I ask this only because now that he's dead I fear we shared nothing ... but I like to think that*

* In keeping with Ed's strategy of toning down the sexual precociousness of his actual adolescence, an account of this first gay night out on the town was left out of *A Boy's Own Story*. Instead, the experience is portrayed in *The Beautiful Room Is Empty* as taking place during the Boy's *college* years.

music spoke to us in similar ways and acted as the source and transcript of a shared rapture. I feel sorry for a man who never wanted to go to bed with his father; when the father dies, how can his ghost get warm except in a posthumous embrace? For that matter, how does the survivor get warm?

Although it is only hinted at in this passage—"I fear we shared nothing"—Ed readily acknowledges today that this image of him and his father rapturously bathing in Brahms together was a wishful fantasy indulged in precisely because he and E.V. "never had any rapport to speak of" in real life. Having begun writing *A Boy's Own Story* in the months following his father's death when he was still "feeling extremely upset, partly because I had ignored him for the ten years preceding his death and only by accident had seen him a month before he died," Ed now experienced a strong impulse to romanticize his relationship with his father, if only to counteract his feeling "the full burden of how unresolved our relationship was and how unfulfilling it had always been."

But for all the romanticizing of E.V., there is nonetheless a genuine air of mystery surrounding E.V.'s passionate attachment to his favorite classical music—and thus an air of mystery around his inner life itself. Nothing in his background or personality would suggest a passion for an emotional art form such as music. He disliked the rest of the arts, for one thing, and otherwise gave every appearance of being a rigorously pragmatic man who cared only about his business, his status, and living well in a material way. Indeed, as a teenager Ed had often found it puzzling "to be listening to this very romantic, emotion-drenched music and here's this totally cold, expressionless man." George Newman remembers that E.V. was so "absolutely mad about classical music" that he would play his records at high volume late at night. One night a neighbor on the far side of Madison Road complained to the police about the noise, prompting an "outraged" E.V. to insulate his upstairs office and install an air conditioner so that he could play his music whenever and as loud as he wanted.

The most grandiose compliment Ed ever paid his father is contained in another striking passage in *A Boy's Own Story*'s opening chapter. Here Ed goes so far as to compare the father to Orpheus, making it sound as though the father had been the Boy's original (and all-important) love object. For in the years after the father divorced himself from the family, the Boy and his mother and sister

> ... *were shadows, like the dead after Orpheus passes them on his way through the Underworld, after this living man vanishes and the last sound of his music is lost to the incoming silence. All my life I've made friends and lost lovers and talked about these two activities as though they were very different, opposed; but in truth love is the direct and therefore hopeless method of calling Orpheus back, whereas friendship is the equally hopeless because irrelevant attempt to find warmth in other shades.*

Part of the explanation for this passage is that as a child Ed couldn't help but become "infected" by his mother and sister's feeling that their earlier life with E.V. had been "this lost golden age"—even though Ed's own life before the divorce was far from golden. Then too, "part of it is this almost Genet-like respect for 'the man'"—the notion, that is, that because E.V. was the biggest, most powerful man in Ed's adolescent world, anyone else was merely "an impoverished substitute." Finally, Ed as a novelist had been influenced by Proust's "disdainful" attitude towards mere friendship: "the only thing Proust really values is love." As an adult Ed has often marveled at how he, Margie, and Delilah have persistently glamorized E.V. through the years, making him larger than life—by turns more handsome, richer, or more sinister. Yet there has also been an equally persistent urge in Ed to defame E.V. He can just as easily speak of his father as having been, for all his love of Brahms and his poetic nocturnal schedule, "a bore," a joyless, deliberate man with a "grin and bear it" attitude towards life—"a real shit." While giving a President's Lecture at Brown University in 1996, for example, Ed gleefully informed his audience that in his novel *Nocturnes for the King of Naples* he'd taken pleasure in transforming his dull father into a glamorous playboy and heroin addict. My own sense sitting in the audience, however, was that this naughty dismissal of E.V. had something of the odor of a for-mer Catholic's thrill in apostasy. (Ed immediately sprang to mind, for instance, when I happened to read in Lyle Leverich's biography of Tennessee Williams—Williams being another gay writer haunted all his life by his father's disapproval—that nothing is quite so damaging to a young male ego as a father's rejection.)

What did remain constant in the mixed feelings Ed would always have for his father was the perception that E.V. was a pow-erful force to be reckoned with. Just as Delilah was someone Ed had alternately wanted to merge with and flee from, E.V. was for years someone that Ed wanted either to escape from or escape *with*. By age fifteen Ed was capable of feeling both urges simulta-neously: "I hated him and felt he was what I must run away from. To be sure, had he pulled the car off the highway right now and turned to say he loved me, I would have taken his hand and walked with him away...."

Ed's belief that "writers usually write best about things they feel deeply about but also deeply ambivalent about" has never been better demonstrated than in his portrait of his father in *A Boy's Own Story*. It is one of the most memorable pas-sages in his writing.

If Ed and his father had little in common besides music and didn't particularly like each other, E.V.'s surprising friendship with George Newman seems to have come much closer to approximat-ing the kind of father-son relationship E.V. would have wanted with Ed. Not just any boy could have related so well to E.V., of course, but George, while ordinary in many respects, was that rare teenager who was as unendingly fascinated with business as E.V. And business talk formed the heart and soul of his friendship with "Mr. White." George was the only person outside of family and business contacts with whom E.V. socialized regularly, and many a night would find George sitting in E.V.'s living room while E.V. expounded upon the intricacies of the accumulated earnings tax among other favorite topics. Other nights Kay might join them for a game of Crazy Eights. Or E.V. and Kay might telephone him out

of the blue from the office and pick him up at nine in the evening
for dinner at a Chinese restaurant downtown—an experience that
George found wonderfully exotic both because of the late hour and
because Chinese food was still a "novelty" in 1950s Cincinnati. Or
they might all go take in a performance of the Cincinnati
Symphony, afterwards going backstage to get the first violinist's
autograph. E.V. and Kay even invited George up to Walloon Lake.

Just as E.V.'s love of music hinted at unexpected depths to his
soul, his friendship with George Newman reveals that even
someone as misanthropic as E.V. could sometimes have a yen for
company. And while it could be said that in George Newman he
had simply found a young, agreeable, nonthreatening male who
provided an ear for his endless monologues on business,
George's affection for him nonetheless goes some way towards
humanizing E.V.'s otherwise forbidding character. Just as
Margie's friend Penny McLeod had found Delilah and her children the most colorful people she knew, so George Newman
found Kay and E.V. intriguingly different and stimulating—
unlike anyone else in his world.

Business might have been his favorite subject but E.V. also liked
talking baseball, though this too was a subject that Ed had
absolutely no interest in. In the opening pages of *A Boy's Own Story*
Ed begins his portrayal of his summer of 1955 with a midnight boat
ride on Walloon Lake during which the twelve-year-old son of
guests strikes up a baseball conversation with the Boy's father.
Helplessly, the Boy watches this twelve-year-old stranger instantly
establish a better rapport with his father than he himself could ever
hope to enjoy. As it happens, however, the Boy soon establishes an
unexpected but far more intimate rapport with the twelve-year-
old—for it was during this summer that Ed had a brief fling with
twelve-year-old "Kevin Cork," as he was called in the novel.
Ironically it was Kevin, an ordinary heterosexual boy who was captain of his little league baseball team, who initiated several nights of
furtive "cornholing" between him and Ed in the Walloon Lake
basement by asking Ed if he were now too old for cornholing
(something that Kevin and his pubescent neighborhood friends had
all recently discovered and were now busily doing to one another).

Masking his inner excitement, Ed casually told Kevin that while it was true that he ordinarily wouldn't be interested in cornholing, in this case he would be up for it if only because there were no girls available.

By posing as a horny heterosexual boy willing to cornhole in the absence of anything better, Ed had temporarily solved (at least outwardly) what would continue to be a dilemma all through his adolescence and early adulthood: how to love men but not be homosexual. For in his cornholing with Kevin, Ed was in effect returning to earlier days when he had fooled around with hetero-sexual boys, whether playing "Squirrel," or cornholing with fel-low campers at Camp Towering Pines and the neighbor boy in Cincinnati. But what Ed found new about cornholing with Kevin was Kevin's unexpectedly exclaiming "That feels really great" while Ed was taking his turn cornholing him. "That was very weird because it had never occurred to me that anybody could enjoy anal intercourse. It always seemed to me that the person getting fucked was just making a big sacrifice." Later, as an adult, Ed "came to love to be fucked, like most gay men," but as a teenager he hadn't yet "eroticized that act."

Although Ed, as jailbait, found it difficult to see more than once the older men he had anonymous sex with, one adult he did see again was a Northwestern student he'd met at another men's room he cruised: a public washroom that somewhat resembled a small Greek temple, complete with columns and cupola, that stood in a park on the lakefront in south Evanston. This Northwestern stu-dent was a handsome Mexican with "big black eyes and this won-derful kind of permanently tanned skin." Of all the men that fifteen-year-old Ed had already slept with by now, it was this Mexican Northwestern student who first kindled real passion in him through their fleeting but romantically charged encounters. Fleeting, because the second time they met (Ed had invited him back to the Sheridan Square apartment, thinking Delilah had gone out for a few hours): "He and I started necking and fooling around and I looked out the window and saw Mother coming back—and I totally panicked. So I spirited him out the back door and he left, and then of course I never saw him again. I was furious with Mother for coming back early and I was furious that I hadn't gotten his number—of course, he wouldn't have given it to me because he would have been afraid to, like everybody was."

Shortly after this Ed did meet a lover that he saw more than twice. Bob Hamilton, a twenty-year-old medical student, happened to be the son of the man Delilah was dating at this time. In fact, Ed had first met the handsome, blond Bob when, in what became in effect a double date, Delilah invited Ed along with "Ham" (as she called her boyfriend) and his son to attend a performance given by the touring Kabuki Theatre of Tokyo at Chicago's Harris Theatre.* From his seat, Ed almost immediately began pressing, then flexing, his leg against Bob's—a bit of "suicidal daring" for which he was soon rewarded with a reciprocal response. This September evening of footsie and Kabuki marks the beginning of what was to be Ed's "fatal autumn" of 1955.

A week or so later Ed hatched a plan to hoodwink Delilah into permitting Bob Hamilton to spend the night in Ed's bedroom. The plan called for Bob, who had no TV at home, to come to the Sheridan Square apartment one Saturday night to watch "The Perry Como Show," drink a bit too much beer, and tell Delilah he felt too tipsy to drive home. Ed's room, with its twin bed set, contained the only spare bed in the apartment. When the plan was put into action, however, Delilah turned out to be unexpectedly reluctant to let Bob sleep over. Finally she relented and Ed spent a romantic night with Bob. The night was romantic both because Bob was affectionate ("the first man who took off his clothes, held me in his arms, looked me in the eye, and said, 'Hey.'"), and because in their sex itself they opted to masturbate each other as opposed to Ed's usual experience of either alternate cornholing or giving an unreciprocated blow job. Sex with Bob was thus "more

---

* Because, again, this was an episode from his adolescence that he deemed too sexually precocious, Ed makes no mention of Bob Hamilton in *A Boy's Own Story*. Only in 1992, ten years after that book was first published, did Ed in his short story "Reprise" write about this crucial affair.

mutually pleasurable because obviously you can jerk each other off at the same time."

Soon after this night of secret sex Ed fell ill with mononucleosis and had to withdraw from classes at Evanston High. When Bob paid a visit to his sickbed, he kissed Ed "long and deep"— something that made Ed feel both "shocked that he, as a medical student, wasn't worried" about catching the disease, and proud that Bob cared enough to take the risk (similarly, when he saw Bob again more than three decades later Bob elected to have sex despite knowing that Ed was HIV positive). Ed's pride in having such a handsome, openly affectionate lover was accompanied by an urge "to confide in someone this wonderful secret that I'd had sex with him"—an urge that had become all the stronger now that "mononucleosis had reduced my world to the size of our apartment and the books I was almost too weak to hold (that afternoon it had been Oscar Wilde's *Lady Windermere's Fan*)."

One night, however, this urge to brag took on memorable and nearly fatal form. For as he and Delilah were cleaning up after dinner she happened to mention that she and "Ham" were thinking of getting married. Ed's astounding response was to tell her "Then it will have to be a double wedding"—with him and Bob Hamilton joining her and "Ham" at the altar!

While the explanation for Ed's dropping this "double wedding" bombshell on his mother would seem to be that, with his self-control weakened by mono as well as the spell cast by Wilde's blithely outrageous sensibility, his pride in having a real lover after years of anonymous sex and unromantic cornholing simply overcame his better judgment—the truth is that to this day it remains something of a mystery to him why these words happened to pop out of his mouth. Interestingly, love had nothing to do with it, for despite his pride in Bob, Ed in fact found him "too cold" to really care about (it was rather the Mexican Northwestern student whom Ed continued to moon over). An alternate explanation would be that Ed was making an unconscious cry for help by, in effect, ratting on himself. And Ed does admit today that along with feeling "very excited" about his affair with Bob he was also "very guilty about it and may have felt at some level that it needed to be denounced."

Whatever its cause, the effect of his "double wedding" bomb-shell was to bring down on himself an "inquisition" in which Delilah pried out of him the full extent of his "homosexual adventures" over the past few years. Delilah then mailed a horrified E.V. a complete report. Although Ed's double wedding quip ultimately resulted in his being sent off to prep school, for a time it looked as though it might ruin his life. For Delilah's first decision was to send him to be evaluated by an Evanston psychiatrist who found Ed to be "unsalvageable" and who recommended that Delilah put Ed in a mental hospital and "just throw away the key." Fortunately, Johanna Tabin, a psychoanalyst who was a colleague as well as a good friend of Delilah's, urged Delilah not to hospitalize Ed. While it's not known how much thought Delilah actually gave to the idea of institutionalization, the great respect that Delilah had for doctors in general suggests that Dr. Tabin's interceding at this point played a crucial role in keeping Ed out of the bughouse.

When Ed returned to Evanston High after recovering from mono—probably sometime in mid-October—he told all the kids that he was dying of leukemia (a bit of news that, apart from serving as a dramatic explanation for his long absence, could also have reflected his feeling that he was actually sick with another disease, homosexuality). Ed's life in Evanston in any event was coming to an end and with it his two-year-long adventure in being rather popular with the local kids.

For all his problems and extended absence from school, Ed still managed to receive full credit for this final semester at Evanston High—both because he'd continued to do course work while laid up in bed at home and because he got high marks on his final exams. Despite his inner turbulence Ed took pains to insure that his high grade point average was maintained, if only because both Delilah and E.V. seemed to see his performance in school as constituting an important measuring stick for just how "salvage-able" he still was. His consistently superior academic achievement consequently must have been another factor in Delilah's deciding not to institutionalize him—as well as something that went a long way towards persuading E.V. to foot the bill for an expensive boarding school.

In telling the story of how he came to go off to the Cranbrook Boys' School halfway through his sophomore year at Evanston High, Ed has sometimes spoken of it as having been his own decision, sometimes as his parents', but in fact it's not clear how the decision was really reached. However the decision was made, the idea of sending Ed to a boys' boarding school was a measure that everyone involved would have agreed needed to be taken in order to arrest his alarming downhill slide into a homosexual fate that had begun the past spring with Sally's rejection and then intensified during the summer and early fall with his encounters with "Kevin Cork," the Mexican Northwestern student, and Bob Hamilton. Enrolling in prep school can thus be seen as mirroring his having gone off to live with his father for a year. For Ed honestly believed (or hoped) that his "imbalance" could be rectified "by entering an all-male world" of a boys' boarding school.

Four

A Homosexual Fate

Having agreed to pay for prep school, E.V. instructed Ed to go to the library, look up various schools, and choose one. So just as Ed had once tried on various eastern religions as though they were clothes, he now read through a guide to private schools as though it were a "volume of future lives." In the end, however, E.V. made the decision himself. Though Ed would have preferred to go to an east coast prep school such as Exeter or Groton, E.V. selected the Cranbrook Boys' School in Bloomfield Hills, Michigan simply because it happened to lie halfway between his Cincinnati and Walloon Lake homes and was thus "a convenient stopover" for him on the ten-hour drive.

When Ed arrived at Cranbrook in January of 1956 to start the spring semester of his sophomore year he found it to be the most beautiful place he'd seen in the Midwest. The five schools on its "baronial grounds" (which included a girls' school and an art academy) had been designed by Eliel Saarinen, who in fact had continued to live on campus until his death in 1950. Yet despite Cranbrook's impressive beauty and despite Ed's being the first in the family to go to prep school, from the start he "saw right through" Cranbrook's pretensions, never doubting that the progressive Dewey-ite education he had received in Evanston's public schools was "infinitely superior." Though Ed would go on to take Latin honors as well as be inspired by a Cranbrook master to major in Chinese in college, he nonetheless felt that Cranbrook was "basically a crammer" that was "several notches intellectually below Evanston High, even though it had all this window dressing of being a kind of fancy English school."

The English public school window dressing included a worship of rugby and an instant tradition of dressing up as "medieval jongleurs" while carrying "a boar's head in at Christmas with an apple in its mouth." The school song even included lines such as Blake's "in England's green and pleasant land"—something that Ed found "entirely insane: they acted like we were in England." The novelist Thomas McGuane, a Cranbrook classmate that Ed would later befriend, felt that it was Cranbrook's need to incorporate "some lost view of English culture transported to America"—complete with the Episcopalian church as a part of campus life—that made the school such "a profoundly dreary place." For behind its pretensions Cranbrook was "dominated by the automotive culture" of Detroit's wealthy suburbs, and the majority of its students were children of the "automobility"—the executives at General Motors, Ford, and Chrysler. Cranbrook was also, as Ed discovered, a "jock" school with "a pretended interest in knowledge and an obsessive interest in sports." The emphasis on athletics was in fact so rabid that at least one adult on campus speculated that Ed's parents must be "monsters" to have sent such an unathletic son to such a sports-mad school.

Although Ed had always suffered in gym class and hated sports, it could also be said that sports hated Ed. He'd once been hit in the head with a baseball, had once vomited in the locker room after having been forced to run a mile, and had—when forced to *swim* a mile at the Culver Military Academy—come ashore more dead than alive, having floundered along, swallowing gallons of water, with his two strokes, the side- and the backstroke. Finally, and most seriously, he'd had his two front teeth knocked out by a golfer's backswing while serving as a caddie one summer when he was thirteen or fourteen. And yet there was also a psychological element to Ed's athletic ineptitude. The Cranbrook track coach once looked on in amazement, for instance, as Ed ably performed a dancing role in *Brigadoon*; afterwards he wondered aloud to Ed why he couldn't bring the same agility and leaping prowess to gym class. "I can do it if I think it's art, but not if it's sports," Ed replied.

Having selected the school for its convenient location, E.V. couldn't have known that Cranbrook, for all its English window dressing, would turn out to be most un-English in its complete lack of homosexual goings-on and thus very much in line with his plan that a boys' boarding school would reform Ed's homosexual tendencies. For Cranbrook, where each boy was given an individual room "to discourage buggery," was so far from being a hotbed of gay sex that Ed never met any other gay boy there (with the exception of one boy he'd known in passing at Haven in eighth grade, Ed wouldn't know a single gay person his own age until college).

Given such uncongenial, even hostile surroundings one would expect Ed's first semester at Cranbrook to have been an achingly isolated one—particularly since Ed had come to Cranbrook already filled with despair about being doomed to a homosexual fate. And in fact this is precisely how *A Boy's Own Story* portrays things. Having lost his "social nerve" as a result of the shattering events of the past year, the Boy's only real social contact in his early days at prep school is with another new boy who has no friends—the eccentric, pro-Nazi "Howie." Only after several long months go by is the Boy gradually able to ease himself into the social world around him. In real life, however, the surprising truth is that Ed began socializing with college students at the neighboring Cranbrook Art Academy a bare month after his arrival at Cranbrook, becoming known as "the Boy who Dared to Cross the Street"—the boy, that is, who dared to cross Academy Row, the street which serves as a dividing line between the grounds of the boys' school and the art academy.*

By taking the bold step of almost immediately befriending a handful of art students—a step that seems to have been unprecedented at Cranbrook, for no one had ever heard of a student from the boys' school socializing with students from the art school—Ed was continuing a pattern begun years earlier of seeking out bohemian adults as the people most apt to understand and appreciate him.

Another pattern that Ed continued in his early days at Cranbrook

---

* These art students do not even appear in *A Boy's Own Story* (which closes with the Boy nearing the end of his second semester at his new school) and are mentioned instead in the opening pages of *A Boy's Own Story*'s sequel, *The Beautiful Room Is Empty*.

was writing declarations of love—although this time his declaration was sent to a male instructor at the art academy who was rumored to be bisexual. Once again Ed wrote his declaration on parchment paper, making another poor attempt at elegant italic script, and once again he was rejected. The art instructor was a young painter named Mr. Pouchet who, while flattered by Ed's interest, was not about to risk a homosexual dalliance with an underage boy in the small and gossipy world of Cranbrook. Pouchet chose not to reply to Ed at all, even after Ed had sent him a second note, because Pouchet was "afraid that any response from me would fan the flame." Pouchet, while "not immune to taking pleasure here and there," did not find Ed especially attractive. With his soft, undeveloped, and unathletic body, Ed was far from being the kind of physical specimen that Pouchet—who was something of a connoisseur of the young male body, frequently sketching the more impressive Cranbrook lads in action on the playing fields—admired.

What Pouchet did admire was Ed's mind. For though he'd thought at first that it was "the most unusual thing in the world" for this sixteen-year-old boy to be mingling with students and faculty at the art academy, as he got to know Ed he saw that such a boy would be unlikely to find friends on his cultural and intellectual level at the Boys' School. Pouchet also sensed something troubled and unhappy in Ed that, when considered alongside Ed's having had the nerve to slip him love notes, led Pouchet to conclude that Ed was both a "very bold and very vulnerable" boy. Of course, having just been rejected by Pouchet, Ed would have been bound to appear at his most vulnerable. In fact, Pouchet's rejection must have made Ed feel for a time that he had been shut out of both the hetero- and the homosexual worlds. After all, Sally's rejection the year before had made him feel shunted off onto the wrong track of homosexuality, and now Mr. Pouchet's lack of interest was denying him even the guilty satisfaction of sinning.

As he had done the previous year, Ed spent part of the summer of 1956 at his father's Walloon Lake summer house. This time, however, the emotional atmosphere was altogether different. For one thing, Ed and E.V. were alone together at Walloon Lake, Kay having stayed on in Cincinnati. More important, it was during this summer, the most difficult Ed would ever spend with his father, that E.V. imposed on Ed a "work program" in which Ed was forbidden to read (E.V. regarded reading as an idle, even character-warping pastime) and made to do endless manual labor. Ed's primary task—"raking the pine needles that formed a thick carpet from top to bottom of the slope on which the house was built"— was something that he would later incorporate into a passage in his first published novel, *Forgetting Elena*:

> *For the hundredth time I survey the hill and calculate how long I'll need to clear it. I expend more energy on these estimations than on actually working, as though I hope to will all the needles away with one powerful thought.*
>
> *... I must stop drifting off into these reveries. What if Herbert's* watching me?*
>
> *... I push my freight of needles up the hill, knowing now to avoid that steep path where I lost my footing the time before, giving wide berth to the above-ground root and the shallow declivity, ascending on an angle, wondering if there is anyone who is my protector, anyone who cares about me, anyone who realizes I'm here, if I could move to another cottage and escape Herbert's tyranny; wondering how I offended him ... wondering if I will be permitted to go to the hotel tonight and the beach tomorrow, or if I am to work here from now on, perhaps sleep here, too....*
>
> *Why have they left me here alone? The work itself is not so terrible, except insofar as I believe it's a form of punishment. It's the punishment that weighs so heavily on me, the punishment and the loneliness and the uncertainty that it will ever end.*

The heavy but mysterious sense of punishment that this passage effectively conveys came about in real life, as described in *The Beautiful Room Is Empty*, because E.V., while adamant that Ed

---

* "Herbert" is an authority figure in *Forgetting Elena* whom one can easily transpose, for my purposes here, into E.V.

finish the impossible task of raking an entire hillside of pine needles, refused to explain what possible purpose was being served.

For weeks we had circled each other wordlessly, my father up on a ladder, me with my eternal rake and wheelbarrow, his anger between us, mysterious as the stone the Muslims worship. Since he knew how to cook nothing but steaks, every night we'd sit wordlessly over plates overflowing with fat and blood. He'd read the newspaper. I couldn't guess why he hated me so much.

It was only when his stepmother showed up at the end of the summer and told Ed privately that he was a "monster" for having so upset E.V. the previous fall (when E.V. had learned about Ed's homosexual activities from Delilah despite Ed's having made her promise not to tell him) that Ed finally realized that the endless pine needle-raking was his father's way of punishing him for his perversion as well as an attempt to work the "homo" out of him: "She said that Daddy was sick over this thing and couldn't sleep." Years later Kay confided to Helen White that Ed's homosexuality had continued to "hurt E.V. a lot" for the rest of his life. And though E.V. had done his best to correct the problem, both through his own programs and by lavishing money on therapists that Ed began seeing, the whole ordeal had been very "hard for him." Thus Ed's double wedding quip resulted not only in his going away to Cranbrook but also altered the course of his summers—for the pine needle-raking summer of 1956 was only the first of what would be two consecutive summer work programs imposed on him by his father.

◆✿

Despite its being a place so unsuited to him, it was at Cranbrook that Ed nonetheless feels his real life began. Here he first began to live as an independent person free of his parents; more important, it was here, during his second semester in the fall of 1956, that he began writing novels. Before graduating Cranbrook he would complete two novels: *Dark Currents* (also called *The Tower Window* but henceforward referred to here by its original title,

Dark Currents) and *Mrs. Morrigan.* Just as the timing of Ed's daring to mix with art students and an art instructor was different from what one would expect, so his timetable regarding the writing of his first novel *Dark Currents* is also surprising. Surprising because Ed has described the writing of this autobiographical first novel, which details the shattering experiences of the previous year that led to his coming to Cranbrook, as something he felt compelled to do in order to save his sanity: "I felt I was drowning in my problems and that only by writing about them could I keep abreast of them." Given these circumstances, one would expect him to be feverishly at work on *Dark Currents* soon after arriving at Cranbrook; after all, this is when his sense of having been dethroned from his dreams of becoming both a heterosexual as well as socially significant person would have been at their height.

Dark Currents was written over the course of several months of "study halls"—the obligatory two-hour evening study sessions during which each student worked at his desk in his room. Unlike almost all other students, who were busy playing sports in the afternoons, Ed usually managed to finish his homework earlier in the day so that he was able to "consecrate" his evenings to writing his novel in his room across the hall from a "handsome science-major type." From the beginning Ed was prone to like what he wrote and regard it as "great," but as he started work on *Dark Currents*, writing on loose sheets of paper, he became so "worried about not going ahead and constantly rewriting (and also I was afraid of losing pages)," that he began to fear he might never finish it. His solution was to write in a bound notebook, which kept his pages in order and obliged him to keep moving forward with the novel. Ed's practice of composing his books both quickly and in longhand in a "pretty notebook"—something he's continued to do throughout his career—is thus something that originated with his very first novel.

Another strategy he came up with to help him finish *Dark Currents* involved a disastrous technical decision he made before beginning his second draft. In his first draft he'd found himself so overwhelmed by reporting all his hero's voluminous thoughts and feelings that he'd come to feel that he "couldn't get the story to move ahead because I was so bogged down; I realized less would be more if I could just get rid of all this junk." As a means of imposing some order on what had been chaos, Ed went to the other extreme, omitting *any* mention of his hero's thoughts and feelings. The result is a disappointingly external and impersonal story in which the hero is seen from an odd distance by an author who can only tentatively guess what his hero might be feeling by observing his outward actions and facial expressions. But while *Dark Currents* is clearly juvenilia, this novel written nearly a quarter of a century before *A Boy's Own Story*, when the story truly was a boy's story, remains an interesting prototype of Ed's best-known book.

Just as Ed had done in real life (and as the Boy does in *A Boy's Own Story*), the hero of *Dark Currents*, "Peter Cross" (a name Ed had selected with the idea in mind that his hero was a Christ-like martyr), sends a declaration of love to a girl with whom he has had but a single date. But when she rejects him, Peter Cross decides to get together again with a man he'd met in the men's room of a lakeside park. This character is directly modeled after the Mexican Northwestern student Ed had been so crazy about; but while in real life Ed had had sex with him once and later taken him back to the Sheridan Square apartment only to have Delilah interrupt things, in *Dark Currents* Peter Cross is far more innocent. Not only has he not slept with the Mexican student but their second meeting takes place on the beach, not the boy's apartment. Nonetheless, it is in this scene on the beach, which occurs near the end of the novel, that Peter Cross becomes so swept away by his feelings for the Mexican student that he realizes in a moment of grand revelation that he is gay.

Ed felt no trepidation writing a novel with a homosexual theme because in certain respects he was and always had been quite bold. Moreover, his going ahead and writing *Dark Currents* despite being acquainted with so few models of gay literature shows, as Ed now proudly points out, "how compelled I was to write this stuff—that I could break through what was generally total silence." Of course, a few contemporary works featuring gay protagonists were available in the 1950s but most of what did exist, such as Gore Vidal's *The City and the Pillar*, Ed didn't yet know about. John Rechy's *City of Night* and Isherwood's *A Single Man* were not published until the 1960s, and—most important of all—Genet's *Our Lady of the Flowers* was not available in the U.S. in English until the 1960s.* Yet bold as Ed was to proceed with his risqué subject matter, he nonetheless did conform to as well as personally believe in the contemporary literary convention that held that writers portraying homosexuals must court the reader's sympathy by offering up an explanation for their hero's tragic affliction. In *Dark Currents* this meant that Peter Cross was "presented as being a victim—that is, because this awful girl had rejected him he was forced to be gay."

The few literary models dealing with homosexuality that Ed was familiar with while writing *Dark Currents* were all very remote (not American, not contemporary): Mann's *Death in Venice*, Rimbaud's *A Season in Hell* (in which he details his experience with fellow French poet Paul Verlaine), and the Nijinsky biography his mother had given him a few years earlier. While Ed had heard about the play based on Andre Gide's *The Immoralist*, he hadn't yet seen it himself or read the novel (and when he did get around to reading *The Immoralist* years later, he found it to be surprisingly tame, ending as it does "with just a hint that—*maybe*—he might be going to do something gay").

Ed had also heard about but hadn't seen the "infamous" Broadway production of *Tea and Sympathy* (a play that Ed still hasn't seen and—interestingly—has continued to misunderstand all these years). For while *Tea and Sympathy* is in reality about a prep school boy who is guilty of nothing more than non-conformism (a penchant for playing female roles in school productions as well

* At the time Ed was unaware of the edition of *Our Lady of the Flowers* "that the beatniks read which was done in France but in English and that wasn't permitted in America; people would bring it in as a traveler's companion." Ed was also unaware of John Horne Burns, whose gay novels had been published in the 1940s but who had to wait until the late 1970s before his work was revived and known to a wider audience.

as for walking too lightly on his feet) who becomes so hounded by false rumors and the other boys' taunts that he himself starts to believe that he must be queer, Ed's notion of the play has always been that the boy "doesn't know whether he's gay or not and the wife of one of the teachers at the prep school decides to sleep with him in order to save him and convince him he's actually heterosexual." In reality, the play ends with the housemaster's wife—the only person on the scene who has never doubted the boy's "manhood"—deciding to sleep with the boy and thus confirm for him what we the audience have known all along: that the poor boy is and always has been healthily heterosexual and has simply been the victim of a very 1950s smear campaign. Thus what's interesting about Ed's long-running misconception of *Tea and Sympathy* is that it would seem to be a projection of his own youthful views as expressed in *Dark Currents*.

If Ed wrote *Dark Currents* with little sense of literary precedent for presenting homosexuality as a theme, he also gave little thought to emulating the style of any literary hero, such as his early passion, Henry Green. "I don't think that I had quite connected in my mind yet that you could imitate writers. I think I was still so bedazzled by writers when I'd read them that I'd lose consciousness of technique." As a result, the quality of the prose in both *Dark Currents* and *Mrs. Morrigan*, the novel he wrote the following year, is quite ordinary and unlike Ed's mature writing in its utter lack of stylishness. For though he continued to write poetry regularly at Cranbrook, prose and poetry were still entirely separate forms for him and the idea of lavishing on a novel the line-by-line attention more commonly reserved for poetry—a quality that would become a hallmark of his adult writing—had not yet occurred to him. "Prose I wrote just as I talked—very spontaneously and without any reflection."

Along with his need to make sense of his personal problems, Ed had also been driven to write *Dark Currents* by dreams of winning attention, praise, and even financial independence. "My fantasy was that I would send it off, get it published, become rich and famous, and be able to thumb my nose at Daddy and Mother." Yet *Dark Currents* ended up fulfilling none of these ambitions, nor even having the chance to, because Ed never bothered to send the novel out to anyone. "I must have been afraid of failure, and probably even more afraid of success." It also seems possible that he was reluctant to show *Dark Currents* to anyone because of its homosexual theme.

Furthermore, by writing a novel that amounts to an apologia for his homosexuality, Ed may have succeeded in making sense of his feelings but in doing so had only strengthened his sense that he was doomed to a homosexual fate. Indeed, his growing alarm about his stubborn homosexual urges led him to decide to seek psychiatric help a few months after finishing *Dark Currents*.

> *I wanted to overcome this thing I was becoming and was in danger soon of being, the homosexual, as though that designation were the mold in which the water was freezing, the first crystals already forming a fragile membrane....*
>
> *In the back of my mind I had kept hoping I'd somehow outgrow this interest in men, an interest I had nonetheless continued to indulge. But now I was becoming frightened. I was being pushed out of the tribe. I had a dream in which I was a waiter in an elegant restaurant where I served happy, elegant couples. That was upstairs. Downstairs the filthy kitchen was staffed by bald, grizzled men, convicts, really, mute, bestial with grief. They wore blood-stained aprons and gleamed with sweat. I was one of them and, although I could rise to circulate among the happy diners, I always had to descend back down to the hopeless workers, each suspicious of the others. And then the police van arrived and the help, all of us, were dragged out into the night ablaze with revolving red lights. We were hauled off to prison, where we'd remain forever. As I was being herded into the van I could feel on my back the eyes of the diners looking down from the windows upstairs. Now they knew I wasn't one of them but one of the convicts.*

But just as Ed wrote his first novel *Dark Currents* later than expected, so his timing in seeking psychiatric help was also more delayed than one might have imagined. He had come to Cranbrook, after all, with the hope that the manly influence of an all-male prep school, along with being away from his mother, would help to steer him into heterosexuality. Yet once it became clear that his homosexual desires remained persistent as ever, the natural thing for him to do would have been to waste little time before turning to a new measure such as psychoanalysis.

In the more logical world of *A Boy's Own Story* this is what happens: after only a few months at prep school, the Boy begins therapy with a local psychoanalyst. In real life, however, Ed waited to begin psychoanalytic treatment until the fall of 1957, when he'd been at Cranbrook for a year and a half. What makes his delay all the more surprising is that—unlike the Boy in *A Boy's Own Story*, whose ongoing homosexuality consists merely of eyeing other boys' bodies in the showers and sending an anonymous love poem to his gym teacher—Ed managed to have a handful of homosexual encounters at Cranbrook. But while the fundamental reason that Ed sought therapy was to try to cure himself of his homosexual urges, in sifting through all that may have gone into his decision to seek psychiatric help at the beginning of his senior year at prep school one also encounters other possibilities (possibilities that will be explored further on) besides his horror about his sexuality, such as jealousy of his mother's new love life, and even mental derangement, that are too plausible—and certainly too juicy—to be ignored.

What is clear is that Ed came to the conclusion that only a psychiatrist could save him during the summer of 1957, just prior to his senior year at Cranbrook. As he had done the past two years, he spent the summer with his father and stepmother in Cincinnati and at the Walloon Lake summer house. At some point that summer Ed, afraid of his father as always, mentioned to his stepmother his desire to see a psychiatrist. Kay then gave him the go-ahead to raise the idea with E.V., who not unexpect- edly refused to "authorize" any treatment. On a brief visit to Chicago at the end of the summer, however, Ed lied to his mother and told her that E.V. had merely said that he hadn't reached any definite decision yet about paying for therapy. A few weeks later, after Delilah had driven him back to Cranbrook for the start of the fall semester, Ed shocked both his parents by deciding on his own to go for an initial session with a local psychiatrist. This provoked a flurry of letters—mainly between Delilah and E.V.—that debated whether Ed truly needed psychiatric treatment and how it might be paid for.

This summer of 1957 had featured another work program that, while not as intensive as the previous year's "pine needle program," did consist of a summer job E.V. had found for Ed at Friedman's (E.V.'s haberdasher), healthy doses of yard work and house painting, as well as a complete ban on the corrupting "frills"—"opera, symphony, plays, special restaurants" and all "adult social groups"—with which E.V. believed Delilah had warped Ed's character. Yet because toiling in yet failing to benefit from his father's programs was nothing new for Ed, one's attention is drawn instead to what was unique to the summer of 1957—namely that Delilah had begun a love affair with a man named Abe that was more impassioned than anything she'd known since she'd nearly married the "good-looking fool" from Kentucky who'd wanted her to buy him a fishing camp a decade earlier.

In "His Biographer," a short story he wrote in the early 1990s, Ed remarks that in biographies "what readers expected and publishers demanded was, quite simply, the key, or at least a scoop. Ideally the scoop, also sexual, would be the discovery of a previously hidden document." Ironically, just as "His Biographer" was being published in America in 1995, some old letters between E.V. and Delilah turned up, written in the fall of 1957 when the idea of Ed's going to a psychiatrist was being debated. In one of these letters—the scoop, as it were—E.V. tells Delilah that when Ed returned to Cincinnati from a brief visit to her in Chicago early that summer of 1957,

> *he was visibly upset because he felt that Abe, your new boy friend, was too young, and because you indicated that you were seriously interested in him. It was on his mind constantly and he discussed it frequently. When we returned* [to Cincinnati from the Walloon Lake summer house], *he had a letter from you, mostly about Abe. He read the letter only partially through, then tore it into bits.*

*Subsequent letters upset him even more, and he became obsessed
with returning to Chicago.*

*... I tried to counter with Ed, by telling him that you were an indi-
vidual just as he, and that you were an adult who had a right to enjoy
life as you saw fit. It failed to compose him, however.*

Ed today claims to have no memory of the incident and
doubts it ever occurred. But because it seems unlikely that E.V.
possessed the imagination to dream up such a story, Ed suspects
that his stepmother suggested it to him and that E.V. would have
been receptive to just such a ploy because it would be to his advantage to reduce Ed's desperate state of mind to being merely a case
of a boy who'd been encouraged to become too attached to his
mother but who could nonetheless learn—through some discre-
tion on Delilah's part along with the continued weaning effect of
boarding school—to make the necessary "adjustments" without
recourse to expensive psychoanalysis.

Of course, it's tempting—even exciting—to speculate that Ed
really did rip up his mother's letter in a fit of jealousy. After all, if
he did in fact do this it would be natural for him to be embarrassed
enough today to drop his usual candor and deny the whole incident. Furthermore, Ed does admit that in the summer of 1957 he
felt no one really loved him but his mother and that one of the
reasons he found the psychiatrist he would soon begin treatment
with so appealing was precisely that this doctor frequently pro-
claimed his paternal love.

It was clear to both Delilah and E.V. that Ed was still overly
attached to his mother. "One night while he was here he talked
for hours telling me all my faults & what a terrible mother I
had been," Delilah confides to E.V. about an encounter with Ed
that summer.

*I listened quietly and in no way took it personally. I felt that perhaps
it was a good move and that it meant at last that he was growing up
& was becoming psychologically weaned from me. Two or three days
later, however, he had a violent quiet reaction to what he had said
to me and feared that he had cut off one of his few emotional ties. He*

became panicked over this, but I reassured him that a mother's love was continuous & not influenced by such situations.

In his reply, E.V. informs Delilah that Ed's lashing out at her "stems entirely" from his jealous rage at her having taken up so seriously with Abe.

You have always treated Ed as an adult. Start treating him as a child, and don't confide anything to him about your personal life. He was sold that your relations with Hamilton were platonic and solely for companionship and security. This did not disturb Ed and would not have disturbed him, even if you had married Hamilton. But he feels that your relation with Abe is different. Ed does not want to share your deep interest with any man. So, with Abe, or anyone, can't you keep Ed's mind at ease by indicating the "Hamilton" convenience, companionship, security angle, regardless of your true feelings?

Granted that Ed is overly "mother-conscious," if you do not aggravate him, in time, he will find and transfer much of this feeling to his girl friend, mature, and drop most of his mother fixation.

If Ed was in fact crazily jealous about being replaced in his mother's heart by her new boyfriend Abe, it would do much to explain the symptoms of mental derangement that, as will be seen, Delilah told E.V. she had observed in Ed that summer. On the other hand, as will also be seen, it's quite possible that this so-called derangement in Ed, like his alleged reaction to Delilah's passionate involvement with Abe, never actually happened.

Another new development in Ed's life during the summer of 1957 was hustlers. With money earned from his summer job at Friedman's, Ed began hiring hustlers he would meet in Fountain Square, which in Cincinnati's small downtown stood just blocks away from Friedman's as well as from Ed's other old Cincinnati haunts: E.V.'s office building, the public library, and the Netherland Plaza Hotel. Of course, that Ed was hiring hustlers at all shows that, as with his early cruising, he could be extremely bold ("I don't know of a single other gay man who when he was seventeen was hiring hustlers"), but hiring them left him feeling more guilty than ever about his homosexuality and triggered an acute sense that his homosexual desires were now truly getting out of control.

In *A Boy's Own Story*'s account of this hustler-hiring summer, the Boy is not seventeen but *fourteen*—a curious reversal in an autobiographical novel in which Ed otherwise strives to make his younger self less sexually precocious. The explanation for this departure from his overall strategy likely had much to do with Ed's tendency to treat the chapters in his novels as separate worlds unto themselves. And the "hustler chapter" (chapter two) might well have taken on a blithe life of its own simply because Ed got carried away writing something that he hoped would get laughs from his new gay audience (what never gets mentioned in the book's lighthearted account of the hustlers is that hiring them was something that considerably disturbed him at the time). In any event, the hustler chapter is what Ed read aloud to the astonishingly large audience of gay men he found gathered to hear him read from his work in progress at the Leslie-Lohman art gallery in New York in 1981.

When Ed made his bold decision in September of 1957 to pay an initial visit without parental permission to Dr. James Clark Moloney, a well-known analyst with an office in Birmingham, Michigan near the Cranbrook campus, Moloney sent E.V. an invitation to discuss immediate treatment.

> *Dear Mr. White:*
> *I have seen your son Edmond* [sic]. *He is desperately anxious to do something about his distorted fixed attitude toward people. He can not do it by himself and needs professional help. He also needs your help. Is it possible for you to come to Birmingham to see Edmond and to see me regarding getting effective and sustaining help.*
> *Cordially,*
> *James Clark Moloney*

Reading Moloney's note all these years later for the first time, Ed was "struck by the fact that Moloney had spelled my first name wrong," although readers of *A Boy's Own Story* who remember Ed's portrait of "Dr. O'Reilly"—a character based directly on Moloney—won't find such a misspelling so surprising; after all, the good doctor could never keep the Boy's friends' or even his parents' names straight, took no personal interest in his patients, and was an extremely poor listener. As for Moloney's intriguingly vague diagnosis of a "distorted fixed attitude toward people," Ed speculates that this would have been "the kind of dust Moloney would throw into Daddy's eyes" because "he probably couldn't say anything about homosexuality and he didn't want to use some word like *psychotic*." In any event, E.V. responded instantly to Moloney's note, informing him that "I will not authorize your treatment of Ed. Perhaps his mother will do so, but this must be done directly by her, and at her expense." In a note E.V. fired off to Delilah the same day, he complains that their son's "bulling ahead anyway is not appreciated by me."

In Ed's literary accounts—both nonfictional (*States of Desire*) and autofictional (*A Boy's Own Story*)—of this critical juncture in his life in which everything hinged on getting his father to agree to pay the psychoanalyst's expensive fees, Ed (or his stand-in, the Boy) writes his father a "blockbuster letter" in which "the word *homosexuality*" is used, "thereby breaking a taboo and forcing two responses from him: silence and the money I wanted." In reality, however, things happened quite differently. For the truth is that Ed, who could be so unusually bold, lacked the nerve to mention or even allude to homosexuality in his letter to his father, as E.V.'s response makes clear:

None of the above relates to your past problem [E.V.'s euphemism for homosexuality], *which you did not list in your letter, except that I hope that the past problem was not basic with you, but only a by-product of the real problem of teen-age adjustments. If the old problem is with you, write me further about it.*

Even with his father inviting him to admit that the "old problem" still plagued him, Ed remained unable to tell him that it plagued him more than ever. Instead, Ed's two letters to his father, far from being blockbusters, tiptoed around the real reason he felt compelled to enter therapy in much the same way that Moloney, with his "distorted fixed attitude toward people" diagnosis, had thrown dust in E.V.'s eyes.* More important, Ed's inability to raise the subject of homosexuality played right into his father's hands and E.V.'s maddening habit of minimizing everyone else's problems. Ed's inability to broach the subject of homosexuality in these letters to his father, even as he desperately wanted to convince him of the need for therapy, provides a vivid example of just how afraid he always was of E.V. In fact, fear of his father might well be the explanation for why Ed waited until he'd been at Cranbrook for a year and a half before seeking professional help.

It was Delilah's letters, not Ed's, that finally got E.V. to relent and agree to pay half the cost of Ed's weekly treatments with Dr. Moloney. In her first letter to E.V., Delilah speaks of "the seriousness of Ed's problem" and "his need for treatment." She alludes to Ed's homosexuality ("the problem that caused us so much concern prior to his going to Cranbrook"), yet dismisses it as constituting "only one of the symptoms of a much deeper personality problem" that Ed has been afflicted with "since early childhood." Delilah warns E.V. that their son's condition is "becoming increasingly serious" and that, indeed, "Ed must have help & he must have it now if he is to prevent going under" because "within the last few months he is beginning to have pre-psychotic episodes" involving "compulsions, hallucinations, fantasies, suicidal ideas, and other things." The cause of these disturbing developments, Delilah suggests, is nothing other than a heroic effort on Ed's part to suppress his homosexual desires. "As far as I have been able to determine Ed is controlling the overt homosexuality but at a

---

* Ed's letters to his father have been lost, and so one can only gather what Ed must have written from E.V.'s responses to Ed and Delilah.

great sacrifice to himself," Delilah writes—a line whose unintentional humor had me and Ed laughing as I read it to him over the phone. "As long as he could act out his problem in that way it served as a safety valve."

Taken at face value Delilah's letter makes Ed sound strikingly crazy at this point. Although it is possible that he suffered a genuine (and very brief) mental collapse during this summer, what seems far more likely is that Delilah, knowing how badly Ed wanted to start treatment and aware that only the most dramatic account stood a chance of making E.V. pay for it, deliberately made their son's condition sound more dire than it was. In this light, it's possible that by "suicidal ideas" Delilah was thinking of the half-hearted suicide attempt Ed had made the year before in his room at Cranbrook. This had occurred when Ed had pricked his wrist with a shard of glass but stopped after drawing only a few drops of blood. The shard had come from a piece of stained glass given him by a Cranbrook Art Academy student named Jim Valentine with whom Ed was "madly in love" but who wasn't interested in Ed. Ed had hung the piece of stained glass in the window of his room at Cranbrook but one day it fell to the floor and shattered. Yet this would-be suicide attempt was not provoked by his unrequited love for Jim Valentine. Rather, Ed—who had a romantic interest in "almost everyone at that time"—pricked his wrist because of a more general despair he felt in his early days at Cranbrook.

As for Ed's hallucinations, Delilah probably had in mind his telling her of a vision he'd once had while meditating, again at Cranbrook, when he actually (so he believed) began to levitate and to feel himself "rising up through this sort of tube."

But for all Delilah's efforts to alarm him in her letter, E.V.—who dismissed all therapy as "bunk" and preached self-reliance in all things—stuck to his guns, offering up what he believed to be the real reasons why their son was seeking psychoanalytic treatment:

Dear Delilah:
I read your letter, received today, with interest as regards Ed. I still feel that Ed can make his adjustments on his own, if he really wants to make them. In seeking M.D. help, I believe that he is (A) seeking

a crutch to lean on (which is bad since he cannot have a crutch for all problems during his life), (B) seeking that "special attention" which he always strives for (which is all wrong), (C) throwing a "scare" into us to better influence his future wants, such as possible interference into your relations with Abe, and to force me to send him to Harvard (against my expressed will, but which he desires with an unsatiable [sic] passion), and (D) because he is investigative as to what makes a psychiatrist ticks [sic], because of his ultimate interest in it, as evidenced by his many conversational references to same.

There may be other and valid reasons, such as his inability to cultivate friends, which he professes to miss on occassion [sic]. He is too young to cultivate adult friends, whom he seeks and to whom you have always exposed him, and he is bored and avoids friends among kids of his own age, which is a fault that he could correct on his own account. Ed seeks an exotic, exciting and extraordinary life and one where he is the center of attention, but he is unwilling to work or wait until he deserves commendation.

What's more, E.V. believed his own summer work programs had already begun to straighten Ed out.

I have discouraged this attitude and seem to make temporary headway when he visits me, by discussion, but mainly by direction, i.e., giving him manual and menial tasks such as yard work, painting house, etc., in which I participate with him, and by getting him a job at Friedman's where he does errands, inventories etc with and like other kids working with him and where he gets no adult or preferential attention.

... I discourage Ed's deep discussions, on everything, and just try to set an example of a plain individual, keeping busy at work, and having only normal interests like sports and menial everyday yard and home-life. *

---

* Interestingly, reading these letters of his father's for the first time touched Ed because they were a revelation that his father's intentions were better-hearted and more rational than he had ever supposed: "Daddy wasn't just cruel, he had a program."

Also evident in E.V.'s letter is his desire to cast the blame on Delilah for their son's problems. For though E.V. had admitted in his letter to Ed that the summer just past must have been a difficult and lonely one for Ed in Cincinnati (he and Kay having "excluded" him in their preoccupation with settling into their new Watch Hill home), in his letter to Delilah it suits E.V.'s purposes to portray the summer in a quite different light:

I avoid taking him to adult social groups, to opera, symphony, plays, special resturants [sic] and all of the frills [i.e., everywhere Delilah might take Ed]. This summer, while here, he got to go only to 1-resturant [sic] with Kay & friends. I kept him at work, at Friedman's & at home. He seemed happy and content, until he made his first trip to visit you in Chicago. He came back to Cinti [Cincinnati] visibly upset, and started to phone you frequently, fret, worry and become uncooperative with me, expressing loss of interest in our new house, yearning for Chicago frills, and worrying about you and your interest in Abe.

... Friedman's job, my frequent work program at 2-houses, failed to interest him. He cooped himself up, to write, and brood.

By boasting of his success with Ed early in the summer before Delilah had once again spoiled him, E.V. ties Ed's "composure and maturity progress" to keeping him away from Delilah's less-than-healthy influence. E.V. goes on to tell Delilah that their son, far from needing a psychiatrist, simply needs to stay at Cranbrook "where he is being weaned from parental influences, and where he is not being subjected to parental matters [i.e., her affair with Abe] which disturb his feelings of security."

While his mother-complex may relate to your individual rearing of Ed, and your seeking his favor, for which the cause may well have been our divorce, but [sic] now I feel that his mother-complex is a result which you can treat more discreetly until maturity makes him more rational. None of this is personal, Delilah, but it expresses my objective analysis of Ed's current dilema [sic].

And yet, for all his insistence that what Ed needed was not therapy but simply to be on his own at prep school where he could learn to fend for himself, within a month E.V. had relented. The odd thing, though, is that Ed's homosexuality seems to have played no part in E.V.'s capitulation. Though Delilah had dared to tell him that the old problem was in fact a current problem, what ultimately clinched E.V.'s help was not the notion of his son's sexuality being in peril but the prospect Delilah raised of having to give up her beloved East Chestnut Street apartment on Chicago's Gold Coast if forced to shoulder alone the financial burden of paying for treatment for Ed.

As an adult, Ed has noted a direct parallel between his having gone to see the minister as a little boy and his beginning psychoanalysis with Dr. Moloney a decade later: in both cases he was desperately turning to an authority for help and understanding. Unfortunately, the two experiences also turned out to parallel each other in that Dr. Moloney, like the minister, completely failed to understand him. With Ed's psychoanalysis, however, the failure in understanding had two sides; for though Dr. Moloney was to prove spectacularly inept in his own right, Ed for his part had come to psychoanalysis hoping it could help him to achieve his understandable yet impossible goal: "to be loved by men and to love them back but not to be a homosexual." As Ed underwent psychoanalysis he simultaneously wanted and didn't want to be cured of his homosexuality, a contradictory attitude he likens today to an overweight person's love/hate relationship with chocolate sundaes, although a better analogy might be that of a deeply religious married man caught in the predicament of an adulterous affair, burning with shame, self-hatred, resolve ... and desire.

Edmund White's autofiction is filled with examples that neatly capture this ambivalence, such as: "I had looked up 'homosexuality' and read through the frightening, damning diagnosis and prognosis so many times with an erection that finally, through Pavlovian conditioning, fear instantly triggered excitement, guilt automatically entailed salivating love or lust or both."

Yet what was unusual about Ed was not so much what he felt but the extremes to which he took his feelings of guilt and desire. While many homosexuals in the 1950s felt compelled to explore their sexuality in furtive encounters even as they believed that what they were doing was "sick," Ed regularly sought out and had sex from the time he was thirteen. And if most homosexuals consequently felt plagued by guilt, Ed—at age seventeen—actually went so far as to insist that his parents pay for psychoanalysis.

Any reader of *A Boy's Own Story* cannot be blamed for wondering how on earth Ed's hero, the Boy, could have remained in therapy for years with a psychiatrist as grossly and comically incompetent as "Dr. O'Reilly"—Dr. Moloney, or "Dr. Baloney," as Ed's friends came to call him back then. The reader must first contend with the doctor's crazy appearance and unprofessional manner: his shoulder-length white hair—"a startling length in those days"; his dress: "a piece of rope to hold up baggy, stained trousers, bare feet in hemp sandals"; and the "dirty hanky he kept pressing to his red, raw face, for though we were still in midwinter, sweat lent an incongruous dazzle to his face." Then there's the doctor's brand of therapy. During the Boy's first session O'Reilly immediately steers him over to a log representing "Mom or Dad as the case may be" that the Boy is expected to have "a grand ol' time hacking away at...." Compounding everything is that O'Reilly is also a bad listener who drinks, pops pills, and dozes during sessions. What's more, "When he wasn't presenting his theories, O'Reilly was confiding in me the complexities of his personal life. He'd left his wife for Nancy, a patient, but the moment his divorce had gone through, his wife had discovered she was dying of cancer. O'Reilly complied with her last wish and remarried her. The patient promptly went mad and was now confined in an institution in Kansas. O'Reilly, to console himself, was throwing himself into his work."

All in all, Dr. O'Reilly is portrayed as being such a complete disaster as a therapist that a reader can find it hard to imagine how he managed to retain any patients.

I've singled out the portrayal of Dr. Moloney in the character of Dr. O'Reilly because although O'Reilly is a bizarre and colorful creature who enlivens the novel whenever he appears on the page, his portrait is a rare instance in Edmund White's autofiction where the characterization is heavily distorted because of Ed's retrospective rage while writing it. This distortion is not in the facts but in the manner of presentation—in how O'Reilly is perceived by the author. Moloney seems to have been every bit as comically incompetent as Dr. O'Reilly is portrayed as being in *A Boy's Own Story*, but in sketching the Boy's relationship with the psychoanalyst Ed continually intrudes his adult self, whereas his usual method in the novel is to include a very convincing re-creation of the world as he had felt it as an adolescent. From the moment O'Reilly appears (when we are told, for example, that "There was nothing about this actor that couldn't be read from the top balcony") it is clear that the doctor is being viewed from a withering, adult perspective and not from that of the desperate, inexperienced, and love-starved adolescent Ed had been. The reason for this slip in Ed's approach is that his anger regarding his treatment at Moloney's hands still burns within him.

This unresolved anger has to do—first of all—with Ed's general rage about all the psychoanalysis he was subjected to in the 1950s and '60s (he had a succession of other therapists after Moloney). In a rare fit of anger over dozens and dozens of hours of interviews, Ed denounced all his former therapists for not being "even as liberal, as it turns out, as Freud himself was." For while reading Marjorie Garber's *Vice Versa: Bisexuality and the Eroticism of Everyday Life* for review*, Ed came across "extensive letters from Freud in which he pooh-poohs the importance of homosexuality. And then you realize that the American psychiatric establishment didn't follow him in that regard—they were much more censorious than he was. I just think, 'Well, the hell with them—why couldn't they have even just been as human as Freud was?' I feel like I was an impressionable boy who was upset, and what I was really upset about was being a teenager and trying to come out in a very hostile atmosphere in the fifties."

* "Gender Uncertainties," *The New Yorker*, July 17, 1995.

Among the feelings that Ed had for Moloney that are left unsaid in the *Boy's Own Story* account is that Ed had actually been "very impressed by him" at first. James Clark Moloney was a highly regarded psychoanalyst who, as the author of articles published in the *International Journal of Psychoanalysis* and the *Journal of the American Psychoanalytical Association*, was recognized around the world in psychoanalytic circles. He had also written several books inspired by the child-rearing practices he had observed while stationed in Okinawa as a navy psychiatrist during World War II. Other vestiges from his time in the Far East were the cockatoos kept in cages on his front porch and the large statue of Buddha on display in his garden despite the complaints of conservative Birmingham neighbors that the word *Zen* inscribed in roman letters on Moloney's Buddha was an affront to good Christians.

Along with being impressed by Moloney, Ed was also charmed by the doctor's personal warmth (Delilah too, on meeting Moloney, felt that he was "an old & kindly gentleman. Very understanding"—although the irony, as will be seen, is that Moloney took to castigating Delilah relentlessly in his sessions with Ed). Moloney's warmth was important to Ed because he felt himself to be very much alone in the world at this time. Whether or not Delilah's infatuation with Abe had intensified this feeling, it now had been nearly two years since Ed, believing that Delilah's influence was something he needed to escape, had put hundreds of miles between himself and his mother by coming to Cranbrook. By having cast himself adrift Ed had made himself very susceptible to Moloney and his "vocabulary of love," for Moloney presented himself as a new parent who not only loved Ed but was good for him—even if this "love" often took the form of the dozing doctor suddenly waking up during their sessions to blurt out, "But goddammit, I love you."

What also can't be overlooked is just how inexperienced, and thus gullible, Ed was regarding psychiatrists. Except for his brief visit to the "horrible Freudian" in Evanston who'd declared him unsalvageable, Ed had had no contact with psychiatrists and thus had no one to whom he could compare Moloney. John Hunting, a Cranbrook instructor who was also being treated by Moloney at this time, confirms that Moloney was "well respected" in his field and that people in the 1950s, moreover, did not yet have an unawed shopper's attitude towards therapists. Then too, Moloney had been recommended to Ed originally by a Cranbrook classmate's psychiatrist father. From the start Ed had quite a bit invested in the very idea of seeing Moloney—both because it had been such a battle to convince his father of the need for therapy, and because Moloney represented for Ed his "first toehold toward independence and sanity."

Not only did Ed have a high regard for Moloney early on but Moloney himself was in better form and mental health at first and had not yet started deteriorating as he would a year or so into Ed's therapy with him. As it turned out Moloney was nearing the end of his career and the personal problems involving his wife's cancer and mistress's madness were now beginning to crowd around him. Yet the final and most devastating reason that Ed remained in therapy with Moloney for so long is that Moloney reinforced Ed's old habit of not trusting his instincts. Because Ed "started from the premise I was sick," Ed was led inexorably "to question everything I thought and did. My opinions didn't count, since my judgment was obviously skewed." This habit of doubting himself in turn helped to sustain his faith in Moloney, for Moloney insisted that any objection Ed raised was actually due to problems within himself and thus illegitimate. For instance, although Ed had detected that Moloney, like E.V., was a heterosexual man so uninterested in other men that he didn't even have male friends, had Ed ever dared to bring this up with Moloney the doctor would have been sure to counter with, "Why are you resisting me?"

While Moloney was not without his Freudian window dressing (in imitation of Freud himself, Moloney's offices were filled with exotic primitive art, for instance, and he did seat himself out of sight of his patient, who reclined on the couch), in practice he was far from being an orthodox Freudian. For one thing he talked too much, freely offering up his interpretations: "As a great man and the author of several books, he had theories to propound and little need to attend to the particularities of any given life—especially since he knew in advance that life would soon enough yield merely another illustration of his theories."

Moloney took as his starting point in his sessions with Ed the standard contemporary view that homosexuality was merely a "presenting symptom" of an underlying "original neurosis." Moloney then went on to theorize that this original neurosis, like all neuroses, had been brought about because "parental love had been so partial and so confusing or so absent" that the neurotic felt compelled to create a parent and child within himself. But trouble results, so Moloney's theory goes, when the neurotic falls in love and can't help but project his parent or child onto the unwitting loved one. Such a projection is bound to collapse, of course, as the individual personality of the loved one emerges and the neurotic finds it increasingly difficult to transfer his own "imago" onto him or her. The neurotic is thus doomed to continually repeat the cycle with fresh lovers with ever more unsatisfying returns. The only cure for this wheel of suffering and delusion, Moloney believed, was for the neurotic "to regress in order to be raised all over again" by the good doctor himself and his "unqualified love." Unfortunately, this theory happened to suit Ed particularly badly because, for him, lovers have always represented not an aspect of himself but an Other. Far from being prone to narcissism, Ed throughout his life has if anything tended to find himself repulsive on a deeper level and to feel himself validated only through the love of a superior Other.

Moloney further theorized that homosexuality could be brought on by what he called "castrating bitch mothers." In fact, each time Ed would say anything remotely positive about Delilah in his sessions with Moloney, the doctor would "roll his eyes, like 'Old Boy, here we go again.'" As early as their first session, Moloney was urging Ed to "defend" himself against his mother by keeping her at arm's length. Weirdly enough, Delilah arrived in Detroit a few days later to meet Moloney, putting herself and Ed up in a downtown hotel the night before the meeting and insisting that they economize by sharing a double bed instead of paying for a more expensive room with twin beds. Weirdest of all, as Ed remembers it, was that the movie they happened to see that evening was *Suddenly Last Summer*—"you know, there it was, all this sexual stuff between mother and son." Back in their hotel room, Ed refused to get in the double bed with Delilah, sleeping instead in an armchair. And yet Delilah, who could be very dense, was so unaffected by having seen *Suddenly Last Summer* that she kept waking up throughout the night to call out: "Honey, come to bed." For Ed this long night was nothing less than a total "nightmare."

But when Ed tried to bring up the awful experience with Moloney in their next session, the doctor simply swept it aside. "That was the problem: he was not there for me."

For all Moloney's unprofessionalism and foolishness, his theories had their benign side in that they didn't regard homosexuality as being any worse than other symptoms of a neurosis. Because Moloney viewed all patients, homosexual and heterosexual alike, as suffering from the same underlying problem of having been underparented, he never became moralistic when Ed would faithfully report to him each time he'd engaged in gay sex. After all, if Moloney had declared instead that "You're deeply disturbed and even more so because you're gay," Ed would have believed it. "But the fact that he said the opposite probably gave me at least some feeling of belonging to the human race, which I think I hadn't really had before."

But the malignant side of Moloney's theories was that they held that even someone such as Ed who practiced homosexuality but was otherwise reasonably well-adjusted, nonetheless suffered from a serious but treatable underlying neurosis. Moloney's insistence that the cure hinged on his personally giving Ed unqualified love made his "total incompetence and inattentiveness all the more ironic and disappointing. Because if he'd said, 'Well, no matter what I say, no matter what I do, the process itself will cure you,' that would have been, in a way, less hypocritical." As it was, Ed found Moloney's "love" hard to reconcile with Moloney's being unable to "remember from one week to the next what I was talking about."

And yet for all this Ed not only stayed in therapy for two years with Moloney, but at the doctor's urging actually increased his number of treatments per month. Even as Ed saw he was failing to get "better," Moloney would insist that "you have to get worse to get better and it's all part of the cure."

While Ed was seeing Dr. Moloney during this senior year at Cranbrook he was also singing the lead in a school production of the Copeland operetta *Down In the Valley*. During rehearsals Ed wrote Delilah that Moloney "has promised to analyze me out of my stage fright"—and though Moloney never did get around to performing this particular therapy, Ed did not really need the service. For as is true of many performers, Ed could be petrified before the show but then, once the curtain had come up, manage to call upon his innate abilities as a ham. After all, by adolescence he was already an experienced performer who, as his sister had noticed, always managed to rise to the occasion—whether it was a piano performance of "The Brook" for his parents' guests, singing a pop standard with the house band in a Kentucky nightclub, or dancing the role of Harry Beaton in *Brigadoon* as well as captaining the glee club at Cranbrook. His classmate Tom McGuane remembers that Ed was not only "a good singer" but also had no difficulty performing before the whole school—whether singing, giving speeches, or engaging in public debates.

Still, Ed was often unusually nervous and neurotic. During this same 1957/58 school year, for instance, Ed attended a staged event at Cranbrook with Margie and Delilah and told them both, "So sorry, I have to sit on the aisle" because he wanted to be prepared to flee the auditorium instantly in case a fit of anxiety swept over him (something which did in fact end up happening; Ed disappeared and rejoined them only a long while later). A similar incident occurred a few years later, in the early 1960s. This time he and Margie were attending a performance at the Metropolitan Opera when Ed, who'd once again selected an aisle seat, suddenly raced out of the building for fresh air before returning some ten minutes later to Margie and the opera. What brought on these anxiety attacks was mainly Ed's longtime habit of involuntarily bobbing his head, which could still plague him from time to time. As Ed's head restlessly began to move, the people sitting behind him would often start hissing with vexation. Then too, Ed was sometimes beset by a general phobia about being in a crowd, a "fear of being jostled by all the people." Finally, Ed may even have been "identifying so much with the performers that I was terrified they'd make a mistake. I was feeling a kind of performance anxiety for *them*."

Whatever its causes, Ed's anxiousness is something that distinguishes his childhood, adolescence, and young adulthood. Indeed, people who have known only the increasingly bear-like Edmund White of late middle age (bear-like not only in his increasingly comfortable bulk, but in his sturdy demeanor) find it hard to imagine that he was ever so neurotically high strung, while those friends who haven't seen Ed *since* his youth often single out his new calmness as being the most obvious change in him.

During his early days of treatment with Moloney late in the fall of 1957, Ed committed an "appallingly heartless betrayal" that resulted in the dismissal of a young part-time music teacher at Cranbrook, Mr. Beattie. It was probably the single worst thing that Ed ever did. The events that led to this betrayal were set in motion when Ed began to suspect that Beattie, who like many jazz musicians was a regular marijuana smoker, was trying to interest some of Ed's classmates in smoking pot. In the 1950s marijuana was still commonly seen as an alien and dangerous drug by middle-class Americans and Ed, who'd always had a good citizen side to him, a side that was full of an "excessive worry about doing everything properly," grew alarmed enough to bring up the subject with Dr. Moloney. Confirming that marijuana was "terribly dangerous," the pill-popping Moloney advised Ed to take steps to stop the spread of marijuana in the school.

As it turned out, Ed ended up not only reporting Beattie to the assistant headmaster but also managing to have sex with the unsuspecting Beattie the same afternoon. This astounding bit of wickedness would sit so uneasily in Ed's conscience that nearly a quarter of a century later, while at work on *A Boy's Own Story* in the early 1980s, he waited until he'd nearly finished the novel before checking to see if he would have the "courage" to include an account of it (*A Boy's Own Story* in fact ends with this betrayal). Yet courageous as he may have been to write about the betrayal at all, the novel nonetheless sometimes soft pedals what actually happened.

In *A Boy's Own Story*'s version of things it is his *first* betrayal. In real life, of course, Ed had gotten the special camper kicked out of Camp Towering Pines five years earlier. More important, in *Boy's Own* there is nothing premeditated about having sex with Mr. Beattie. Instead, the Boy hits upon the idea of giving Beattie a blow job purely as an afterthought and through an accident of circumstance; after trying to see the headmaster and being told to come back later, the Boy runs into Beattie by chance and spontaneously decides to seduce him. In real life, Ed's having sex with Beattie was very much premeditated. While it's true that his initial idea had been simply to save the school from "this terrible drug menace," Ed then decided that the situation presented a golden opportunity to have sex with Beattie just as he was about to be fired. Thus, though Ed's original plan to report Beattie to the school authorities was an example of the "witchhunting spirit of the '50s," it was when he hatched the additional idea of having sex with Beattie, knowing that Beattie would never be able to breathe a word about it, that Ed crossed a line and became truly wicked. This all came into play one afternoon while Ed was turning over in his mind whether or not Beattie should be turned in. He was playing the piano in the school's music room when Beattie—a self-styled "White Negro" hipster, as Norman Mailer famously defined it—happened to drop by, mentioning to Ed that one of his jazz musician friends would be coming to visit Cranbrook for a few days. Ed, emboldened by what he perceived as a certain sexual looseness in Beattie, asked him if he and his jazz friend "ever got up to anything?" Asked what he meant by that, Ed replied that he would be interested in "partying" with Beattie himself. With fatal carelessness, Beattie took Ed up on the idea and suggested they get together late that afternoon when the building would be deserted. Having fixed a rendezvous with Beattie for six p.m. in the music building, Ed went at four p.m. to denounce him. This accomplished, he coolly kept his rendezvous with Beattie, gave him a blow job in the music building, then went off to have dinner knowing that Beattie's days at Cranbrook were numbered.

At the end of *A Boy's Own Story* three theories are offered by way of explanation for the betrayal. One theory is that it was a revenge on all the heterosexual males who didn't love him: "Sometimes I think I liked bringing pleasure to a heterosexual man (for after all I'd dreamed of being my father's lover) at the same time I was able to punish him for not loving me." In a larger sense, this wish to exact revenge can be seen as having to do with the homophobic society of the 1950s and its having created in Ed someone filled with self-hatred and twisted resentments. For while it's true that as a teenager in the 1950s—and as a young adult in the 1960s—Ed did not believe that he was oppressed by society, he nonetheless "felt those energies" subconsciously (which explains how he was able to respond so immediately to the groundswell of gay pride unleashed by the Stonewall Uprising in 1969, something he participated in, even though at that time Ed was still in therapy trying to go straight). While Ed blamed himself as an adolescent for his sick homosexuality, he also churned with "all this misplaced energy and complicated resentment of everyone, but unjustified in my own eyes."

On the other hand, very few of Ed's gay contemporaries committed similar betrayals. Rachel Scott—who with her husband, DeQuincey Scott, a Cranbrook master, had befriended Ed at Cranbrook—points out that "the '50s were horrible for everyone, yet millions of people came of age then, including countless numbers of young homosexuals, quite able to love, without ever feeling the slightest need to betray people who had been kind to them and trusted them." In this view Ed's habit of betrayal was not so much something homophobic society had created in him as it was his own personal vice, part of what Rachel Scott sees as his "demonic side." Indeed, Scott's notion of Ed's "mean-spirited" betrayals as being rooted in his demonic nature was confirmed, if not created, by Ed's extremely mocking and unflattering portrait of her in *A Boy's Own Story*.

What can't be lost sight of, however, is that beyond any need to

revenge himself on heterosexual males who didn't love him, heterosexual males were also the only males available to Ed at
Cranbrook. The little sex Ed did manage to have at Cranbrook—
what he calls his "two big catches"—was gained through trickery
or outright extortion. His first catch was a classmate dangerously
close to flunking out of school. In an incident that gives new meaning to the term *dictation*, Ed "told him that I would dictate a paper
for him that he needed to do and that might save him. I dictated the
first half of it and then I said, 'You've got to let me give you a blow
job or else I won't finish the paper.' Horrible blackmail. And so he
did but he just was furious the whole way. And it was strange
because his cock was hard as a rock, so he was obviously into it in
one way, but in another it was so against everything he stood for
and wanted in life, so it was really like rape."

Ed's other big catch was a "very, very handsome and narcissistic blond" with whom he had become friendly in gym class and
whose father was a prominent Michigan politician. "One night I
came down to his room and I sat on the edge of his bed—this was
after Lights Out, which was strictly forbidden—and I told him
that there was this fourteen-year-old kid who would come to my
room every night and give me a blow job. I said, 'Would you like
me to send him to you?' And he said, 'Yeah, that'd be great.' So
then I said, 'Well, it's actually me. And I'll give you one.' So he was
really excited, I gave him a blow job, and then he wanted me to
come back and do it again but I felt too guilt-ridden."

Another reason that Ed never went back to the politician's
son's room was that he'd made the mistake of gleefully informing
his adult friends DeQuincey and Rachel Scott of this latest seduction. Ed was in fact awash in the same mixed feelings that had led
to his boasting about a "double wedding" to Delilah after he'd had
sex with Bob Hamilton: "On the one hand I was very excited that
I'd made a conquest with such a handsome boy and was bragging
about it, but on the other hand I felt very disturbed. There was no
way to justify one's homosexual interests in those days." And much
as his big mouth had gotten him into hot water with Delilah, so too
were the Scotts horrified by what they heard about Ed and the
handsome blond. For not only were the Scotts devoutly religious,

but DeQuincey himself had been homosexual earlier in his life before being "saved" by a priest. Thus DeQuincey sympathized with Ed only so long as he played the "suffering penitent"; but to "go around spreading my satanic activities to innocent boys" was to be "committing evil." The Scotts were in fact so disturbed by what Ed had done that they threatened to report him to the school authorities—"they told me I was virtually a criminal and that I had destroyed this boy's life." Only when Ed begged them not to and promised never again to do such a thing did they relent.

Interestingly, Rachel Scott remembers Ed telling her and her husband that he had been seduced by *Mr. Pouchet*, the art instructor who had not even responded to Ed's written declarations of love. This outlandish claim led Rachel Scott to speculate that Ed was on a perverse and destructive mission to "out" other men in general, and to get himself and poor Pouchet thrown out of Cranbrook in particular. Ed himself has no recollection today of ever making such a claim, but even if he had told the Scotts that Mr. Pouchet had seduced him it seems far more likely, given what we know of Ed's occasional urge to brag, that such an imaginary seduction would have had more to do with vanity than any impulse toward self-destruction—much as the young Truman Capote was fond of complaining (preposterously) that famous heterosexual men such as Albert Camus and Errol Flynn had tried to seduce him.

Another theory offered at the end of *A Boy's Own Story* regarding the betrayal is that it was a revenge on adults in general. Throughout the novel the Boy is portrayed as undergoing not only the oppression suffered by homosexuals but the general oppression undergone by all young people at the hands of adults. But as slaves have sometimes been known to emulate their tyrannical masters when given a chance, the Boy has learned from his oppression to become an oppressor himself, and his betrayal of Mr. Beattie is thus offered up as being a rite of passage into "the tenacious wickedness of the adult world."

Beattie was ... a stand-in for all other adults, those swaggering, lazy, cruel masters of ours (how refreshing it was that ... the teachers were actually called masters). I who had so little power—whose

triumphs had all been the minor victories of children and women,
that is, merely verbal victories of irony and attitude—I had at last
drunk deep from the adult fountain of sex.

Seen in this light, Ed's betrayal of Beattie would seem to be the fulfillment of a nearly lifelong desire to exercise some "adult" power of his own. Yet a convincing argument against this notion is that Ed, far from having been completely powerless, had in fact participated in most of the major decisions of his youth—from deciding to live with his father in Cincinnati, to going away to prep school, to entering expensive psychoanalysis. Moreover, Ed admits that in *A Boy's Own Story* he gave the Boy much more overt feelings of rage towards adults than he himself remembers feeling. In fact, it was only after Ed had found the courage to end *Boy's Own* with an account of his betrayal of Mr. Beattie that he then decided to foreshadow the betrayal by going back through the manuscript and inserting lines such as: "I wanted someone to betray"; or "my fondest if most dangerous fantasy, the one in which I'd no longer be the obliging youth but the harsh young lord ... my older lover helpless, betrayed." In reality, Ed had never consciously fantasized about wielding a cruel adult power: "it was one of those phony things that you put in."

But while it may be true that Ed was not without some power as a teenager and did not burn to avenge himself on adults, he had undeniably suffered an unusual amount of pain at the hands of his parents—each a powerful, oppressive personality—whether it was feeling forced to be married to his mother's despair as a little boy or, later on, to endure his father's work programs and punishment. Ed had long viewed his parents as both being regularly "out of control and crazy"; so much so that as a fourth grader he had written an essay arguing that children, not adults, should be the only group qualified to vote because children were free of the economic self-interest that swayed adult men and the susceptibility to a candidate's looks that influenced adult women.

The third theory offered in *A Boy's Own Story* regarding the betrayal is that he "seduced and betrayed Mr. Beattie because neither one action nor the other alone but the complete cycle allowed me to have sex with a man and then to disown him and it; this sequence was the ideal formulation of my impossible desire to love a man but not to be a homosexual." This impossible desire is, of course, something that Ed had been trying to fulfill for years in various ways, whether it was having sex with the special camper and then trying to send him down the "trap door beside the bed" by denouncing him to his mother; or by pretending merely to be Steve Turner's best friend; or by posing as a horny heterosexual boy forced to make do with cornholing with Kevin Cork. Alone among the theories offered at the end of *A Boy's Own Story*, this is the one that rings completely true.

A Boy's Own Story closes on a perversely jaunty note with the Boy, having successfully seduced and denounced Mr. Beattie, "humming a little tune" as he strolls off to dinner. In real life, far from feeling such callous sangfroid, Ed was "shaking" as he walked along: "I was very nervous that it wasn't all going to come off." And in fact the whole business became far messier than Ed had ever imagined. He had denounced Beattie just before the long Thanksgiving weekend and had expected to find him gone when he returned the following Monday. But to his horror the school administration decided to allow Beattie to finish out the semester and stay on until Christmas break. A further horror occurred when Beattie was told the identity of the student who'd charged him with promoting marijuana use among the boys and Ed was forced to respond to Beattie's countercharge that Ed had been conducting a homosexual relationship with DeQuincey Scott, the Cranbrook master with the gay past (nothing came of this countercharge).

Just as denouncing the special camper had resulted in Delilah's turning her suspicions upon Ed himself, his attempt to save the school from a drug menace ended up making the Cranbrook administration suspect that *Ed himself* had a drug problem. The school, in fact, went so far as to notify the FBI, who in turn sent an "operative" to interview Ed. But instead of being asked for more intelligence about the school's marijuana problem, Ed found himself being lectured to by the operative who had become increasingly convinced that Ed was hooked on pot. An end to the story with Beattie came only three years later. Ed, who was by now a college student at the University of Michigan, happened to enter a jazz club in Ann Arbor one night and was shocked to see Beattie up on stage, performing with a band. Although they didn't exchange a word, Beattie clearly recognized Ed and as their eyes locked for a moment Beattie's eyes were full of hate.

❧

The person who took Beattie's dismissal hardest was Ed's friend and classmate, Tom McGuane. The future novelist had gotten to know Beattie better than any of the boys at Cranbrook because Beattie, a professional jazz percussionist, had been giving him regular drum lessons. But what Tom found particularly endearing about Beattie was that he, alone among the Cranbrook faculty, had "leveled with kids" and made himself "accessible." As someone who resented the "on-high approach to teaching" taken by most Cranbrook masters, Tom thus found it a cruel irony that "the one guy who tried to break through got busted."

Also ironic was that Tom never found out that it was his friend Ed White who'd gotten Beattie busted. Then too, the bust was completely unfounded. For contrary to Ed's belief that Beattie had introduced Tom and others to marijuana, Tom and the other boys never touched any drugs at Cranbrook. The truth was that marijuana had such a dangerous aura about it in the 1950s that even a "racy" teen such as Tom never "dared do it." But when the Cranbrook administration told Tom that they'd discovered the drug "situation" on campus ("we've had an informer"), they refused to believe him when he insisted that there was in fact no drug use going on among the students. For though there was no evidence, beyond Ed's word, of Beattie's having tempted students into smoking pot, the word of an honor student such as Ed carried far more weight than that of a struggling student such as Tom who, as a campus "troublemaker," had already been living in "peril of getting kicked out of school—they were always suggesting I transfer and go someplace else."

It was because he was so consumed with worry about being thrown out that Tom never spent much time wondering who had ratted on Beattie. When the "crackdown" had at last blown over,

Tom only felt relieved that he hadn't been expelled. Because he never learned that Ed was to blame, Tom's friendship with Ed was unaffected by all these events.

Another classmate that Ed had befriended, the future journalist Raymond Sakolov, found it astounding that Tom McGuane and Ed White were friends at all, representing as they did "opposite poles." Tom, after all, was the Irish Catholic bad boy whose rowdy escapades were often gossiped about by the other boys at Cranbrook. Tom, moreover, had no literary or intellectual pretensions at this time—the occasional columns he wrote for the school paper were done in the style of *Mad* magazine—and there were no signs whatever of the distinguished novelist he would become. Ed, on the other hand, was far and away the most cultivated and sophisticated of the 360 boys enrolled in the upper school. Whereas Tom would choose to write an essay on guns for English class, more or less lifting his material from a drugstore novel, Ed wrote about "The Madame de Sevigné Theme in Proust."

Yet what the sensible and admittedly "mainstream" Raymond couldn't have known was that Ed had long been fascinated by rebels and wild boys. Or that Ed's appetite for dabbling in widely different worlds—whether it was adult art students across Academy Row, hillbilly hustlers, or fellow intellectuals such as Raymond—was an integral part of his makeup. And it was characteristic of Ed to act quite differently in his separate friendships. For instance, whereas he dreaded Tom's finding out who had ratted on Beattie and brought about the campus crackdown, Ed not only proudly confided to Raymond that he'd had Beattie dismissed, but even added that it was he who had called in the FBI! Raymond, far from being shocked, listened approvingly since he'd found Beattie to be such a seedy character that he was convinced he must be a junky. Raymond came from the kind of cultured Jewish home that Ed admired and perhaps because Raymond, like Ed, was one of Cranbrook's rare eggheads, he found that their friendship took the form of an ongoing, no-holds-barred intellectual dispute in which Ed would often act "contemptuous and dismiss a lot of my ideas."

With Tom it was just the opposite. For though Ed had once snob-bishly dismissed Tom's Catholic background by telling him, "Once a Catholic, always a Catholic, Tom," as though Catholicism were "a kind of low-rent thing," in his day-to-day friendship with Tom, Ed was full of warm encouragement and praise.

Tom McGuane in fact credits Ed with helping him come to believe in himself as a writer by helping him to overcome his feelings of humiliation at being an academic failure. Ed's most attractive quality was his being a "brilliant person" who was interested in "drawing your intelligence out rather than defeat-ing your intelligence—a very rare thing." Ed for his part found that while his literary discussions might be more "reverential" and high-toned with his adult friends DeQuincey and Rachel Scott, his conversations with Tom were more worthwhile. While Tom was not "particularly cultural," he was "extremely intelligent" and the discussions the two had about writing would be on the order of whimsical yet practical shop talk such as: "Hey, wouldn't it be neat to write a narrative in which you change the point of view every other paragraph?" The Scotts, on the other hand, were friends of the poet Karl Shapiro as well as "under the spell, for religious and cultural reasons, of T. S. Eliot" and with them Ed read and discussed Eliot's religious poems, such as "Ash Wednesday."

Before meeting Ed, Tom had been interested strictly in "adventurist literature"—Conrad, W. H. Hudson, Kerouac and the Beats—and had been particularly drawn to Hemingway's early short stories and novels. "As an insecure Irish Catholic boy I saw Hemingway as a sort of bully Episcopalian figure—the kind of people my dad wished I was more like." But after coming under the influence of Ed and his interest in "depraved European liter-ature," Tom began to read Mallarme, Wilde, and Proust. This taste for rich literary style acquired during his friendship with Ed has continued to coexist with Tom's original preference for more "austere" writing throughout his writing career.

Ed's friendship with Tom McGuane is also interesting in that each fell for the other's bold front; that is, each believed the other to be far more self-assured than was actually the case. McGuane today, for instance, finds *A Boy's Own Story*'s portrayal of him in the character of the fiendishly carefree "Chuck" to be indicative of Ed's having "bought" at Cranbrook "some of what I was trying to sell." For the teenage Tom McGuane was privately "much more timid and insecure" than the outrageous Chuck who, confident in his own genius and unassailability, torments his teachers because he knows they can't touch him. On the other hand, Tom never suspected at Cranbrook that Ed was ever anything less than the "very confident person" who took pleasure in speaking and performing before the whole school.

While Ed made no secret of his sessions with Dr. Moloney, there were no outward signs of the intense anguish that had led him to begin psychoanalytic treatment in the first place. Instead Tom gathered that Ed regarded Moloney as "his great adversary" and their relationship as "a duel of wits." Ed would say, "Moloney's trying to make me do this, but I know better," for instance; or "Moloney's not going to fool me." But while Tom never met Moloney, Raymond Sakolov met "the great James Clark Moloney" several times during the following year when Ed, by then a freshman at the University of Michigan who drove up twice a week from Ann Arbor to see Moloney, would arrange to meet Raymond, now a senior at Cranbrook, at Moloney's office. While Raymond waited for Ed to finish his session, he would be asked to take Moloney's pet monkey out for a walk around the neighborhood.

Amusingly, while Tom McGuane did find Ed to be "neurotic-acting" at times, he attributed this to Ed's "vanity," since being slightly "nuts" was seen as one of the "marks of the chosen." Ed's homosexuality, which all his friends at Cranbrook were aware of, was another eccentricity that if not quite a mark of the chosen was nonetheless accepted as being an inescapable part of the landscape of high culture. There were no fag jokes or queer bashing at Cranbrook, McGuane believes, because the cultural aspirations shared by Ed and Tom's circle helped to promote the idea that just as one should respect good books and pieces of music even if one didn't particularly like them, one should also tolerate homosexuality. "Somehow the idea of trying to grow up to be cultivated people precluded this kind of coarseness."

Despite this cultivated tolerance, Tom nonetheless arranged for Ed to go along on a visit to a Detroit whorehouse. Just as a few years earlier Steve Turner had taken a stab at curing Ed, Tom's thinking was that "Ed has this ailment, which is that he's gay. We'll just take him to the whorehouse and cure him because this heterosexual deal is really lots of fun." The whorehouse, called Aunt Fanny's, was located in a large old house in a rough neighborhood near downtown Detroit, off Woodward Avenue. The boys at Cranbrook had become aware of Aunt Fanny's after a classmate, the son of a local automobile executive, had had his sexual initiation there at the suggestion and expense of his father. Ed's own planned heterosexual initiation at Aunt Fanny's, however, never quite came off. Having selected "Bubbles," an enormous black whore, because he identified with her as a fellow outcast, Ed found himself so unaroused that he was unable to work up an erection. (What *would* be exciting, he realized, would have been to hide in the closet and watch his classmates going at it with their whores.)

Ed had gotten off on the wrong foot with Bubbles from the start when he mistakenly called her "Nipples," provoking the infuriated Bubbles to exclaim: "I ain't no Nipples, I'm Bubbles!" Although they didn't have sex, Ed paid off Bubbles to keep his failure a secret from the other boys. Tom nonetheless sensed that heterosexuality wasn't Ed's "thing" after all, and never asked him whether the whorehouse had helped him to see the light. Raymond Sakolov, who didn't go along to Aunt Fanny's, did ask Ed what it had been like. "It was like jerking off inside someone," Ed replied.

For all his inner anguish, Ed outwardly gave every impression that he wasn't particularly tormented about his homosexuality. Ed had instead struck Tom McGuane as being such a confident eccentric that years later, in the 1960s, Tom was astounded to hear that Ed was now leading the conventional double life of the closeted homosexual in New York. In the honors English class that Tom and Ed both attended during their senior year at Cranbrook, Ed showed no hesitation in reading aloud long passages from his novel-in-progress, *Mrs. Morrigan*, which Tom found to be "a blizzard of dicks." As the class listened while Ed "lovingly described penises for thirty pages," Tom and others would all roll their eyes and say under their breath, "Oh god, here he goes."

Presiding over this English class was an extremely eccentric Cranbrook master named Mr. Wannberger, whom the boys called "the Wombat" behind his back. "The Wombat was hopeless," Tom recalls, "blowing his nose on his tie or tromping around with his foot in the wastebasket. As a result, those of us who were sort of bookish boys probably got as much influence from Ed as we did from the teachers. Ed was far in advance of the rest of us culturally and intellectually. I still think he was the smartest person I ever knew. We were kind of in awe of that." The Wombat, as it happened, was more shocked than anyone by *Mrs. Morrigan*'s graphic sex scenes. Ed, for his part, was "shocked that he was shocked. I thought that we were all beyond that sort of thing. But he kept saying, 'Whoa, eeh, wow, that's pretty heavy stuff there!' Everybody was giggling and gasping. I guess I realized then that you're supposed to present life in a more proper way on the written page. The same people who'd use swear words in conversations would be shocked when I used the same words on the page. And I never could understand that discrepancy. But it is still one that carries today. I think it comes from the fact that writing was originally sacred."

Interestingly, the Wombat once told John Hunting, the Cranbrook instructor who was also seeing Dr. Moloney, that while Tom appeared to be the screw-up and Ed the prodigy, he felt it was Tom who was in fact the more talented one.

Ed finished *Mrs. Morrigan*, which served as his senior thesis, in February of 1958. *Mrs. Morrigan*, which Ed would later turn into a play, is about a few days in the life of a woman going mad after her divorce. Although the character of "Mrs. Morrigan" is based broadly on his mother, Ed's heroine is both a more stylish and more wildly carnal woman than Delilah ever was, the "blizzard of dicks" Tom McGuane remembers being part of her vivid adventures in rough sex, something that Delilah was never interested in. For *Mrs. Morrigan*, unlike *Dark Currents*, has much more to do with fiction than fact, and the interesting thing is that in his first two novels Ed already displayed what would come to be the two basic instincts of his adult writing: the purely confessional on the one hand, and on the other "a kind of projection of essentially myself into imagined lives, into different kinds of people."

After having been professionally typed (though Ed was a more-than-adequate typist himself, he already had the elevated sense of self that such work was beneath him), *Mrs. Morrigan* was ready—as *Dark Currents* never had been—to be sent out. Through friends, Delilah found an agent willing to take a look at the manuscript. The agent, however, pronounced *Mrs. Morrigan* unpromising and passed on it, provoking the eighteen-year-old Ed into an amusing display of hauteur. As he writes his mother:

> *About the agent: glad that he will send book on. However.... Don't take too seriously anyone's opinion about it. For an artist as gifted as I am almost all criticism is valueless. The purification and tightening of my style comes from me alone, or from the brilliant company I keep—my reading of great authors like Proust, Mann etc. My work will never be popular; it's too obscure and minute. But I couldn't and wouldn't write differently.*

This Olympian arrogance, while containing some blunt truth that the artful Ed of later years would never be caught dead revealing, was also a way of "preparing her and myself for eventual failure. Mother's approval of me was very important and yet I felt that Mother was very faithless in that she didn't trust her own opinion and if a professional person said it was no good, then she would think it was no good too."

Ed sent the typing bill on to Delilah, reminding her that she'd promised to pay for it as a graduation gift. "Do *not* pass it on to Dad," he warns—though Delilah proceeded to try to do just that. E.V., however, sent the bill back to Delilah, saying "I don't want any part of it, since we offered to bear the entire expense originally. Kay agreed to type it for him, or have our office help type it during intervals of spare time. It precipitated a major argument, since Ed would have none of it." What his father, mother, and stepmother didn't know was that Ed didn't want E.V. or Kay to lay eyes on the manuscript because he worried that they would mistake the character of Mrs. Morrigan for Delilah—something that would further tarnish Delilah in their eyes.

The wrangling over who would pay the typing bill was just the first of three awkward situations involving Delilah and E.V. that spring. As it happened, June of 1958 featured two important family events within weeks of each other: Ed's graduation from Cranbrook (where he would graduate second in his class) and Margie's marriage to my father, Roy Fleming Jr. The problem was that Delilah and E.V. hadn't so much as spoken to each other over the phone, much less seen each other in person, in the eleven years since their divorce, and Delilah in fact so dreaded catching even the most momentary glimpse of him that, through the years, whenever she happened to be dropping off the children at E.V.'s house in Cincinnati she would insist on their getting out of the car a good block away, a whim that would force Ed and Margie to go the rest of the way on foot, struggling with their heavy suitcases. E.V. too felt so deeply uneasy about their seeing each other in the flesh that the very idea of appearing together at an event, even if this meant sitting at opposite sides of the aisle for once-in-a-life events such as their son's graduation and their daughter's wedding, was unthinkable.

Such an impasse required sensitive negotiations, particularly since it looked as though E.V. would not be attending Margie's wedding. "I'd send you an invitation to my commencement," Ed writes his mother, "but I think that since Dad has some hard feelings about the wedding, I should be free to give him all my attention at this affair. I wouldn't be able to visit you at all—and the ceremony is a bore I wouldn't want to wish on you." E.V. had hard feelings about Margie's wedding because she'd chosen to hold it in the Chicago suburb of Evanston (Delilah's turf) instead of with him in Cincinnati. But no matter how much Margie tried to explain to him that practically all her friends were in Evanston—that she was afraid no one would come were the wedding held in Cincinnati—E.V. remained adamant that he would not attend if it were held in Evanston, and all Margie's pleas fell on deaf ears. Today, more than forty years later, Margie still feels upset that her father found himself unable to come to give her away.

♥

Once this awkward June was behind him, Ed had a delightful surprise in store for him at Walloon Lake that summer. After having suffered his father's work programs and been a lonely misfit at Walloon Lake during so many previous summers, Ed now knew the sweet triumph of achieving a sudden and unexpected social breakthrough there. This sense of triumph also had its unbecoming side, however, for a letter to his mother reveals that his eyes were filled with dollar signs as well as stars:

> *At Walloon I had the most marvelous time. I've met all the kids within a fifty-mile radius of the lake—and what kids! I'm really moving up in society. Gary Randall, whose Dad owns Champion Paper Works (they're billionaires!), invited me to a party at their house; Anne Lottspeich, whose grandmother started Lottespeich's here in Cincinnati; I took out Chip Wilson, C.E. Wilson's granddaughter (a millionairess in her own right); Anne Minor, whose father is one of Cincinnati's wealthiest (they have 70 acres in Indian Hill!) doubled with me one night—gentlemen and debutantes all. I had a luncheon at our house for a few close friends, and we all went water-skiing. I learned how to water-ski!*

Ed's success at Walloon Lake inspired him to envision a similar social breakthrough back in Cincinnati this same summer. Bolstering his hopes was that he had enlisted the help of Betty Herschede, a friend of his stepmother's and a member of one of Cincinnati's prominent families as well as a longtime social leader. It was Betty Herschede who had been instrumental in Kay's own climb up the social ladder, helping Kay to gain membership in Cincinnati's most important women's clubs, such as the Queen City Club. Now that Ed was attempting to follow her into Cincinnati society, Kay—who had been pleased by Ed's social success at Walloon Lake—was more than happy to work with him "hand in glove."

As it turned out, however, even the eminent Betty was unable to launch Ed socially. Despite being introduced to some of Cincinnati's finer families and even being fixed up on a few dates with local debutantes ("Tomorrow I'm going to the opera, *Faust* (2nd row center seats), with Margot Hall, Edmund Hall's daughter"), Ed never became anything more than an uncomfortable outsider at debutante balls. Much of this was simply due to his lacking the time needed to make any real inroads into such a small and clannish high society. George Newman, who dated many debs, including Betty Herschede's daughter, and was very much an insider on the local social scene, confirms that it almost always took years, as it had taken Kay years, for newcomers to make their way socially into Cincinnati's "conservative" world of old families.

Although E.V. took so little interest in social life that he apparently never even bothered to meet any of Kay's society friends, he nonetheless did "dimly approve" of Ed's hobnobbing with the children of the local elite if only "because he knew there was money and power behind those names." And while E.V. never went so far as to say that Ed should marry strictly for money, he did offer the pithy advice to "Just make sure the girls you go out with are all rich." It also seems very likely that E.V. hoped that Ed's interest in debutantes meant that the "old problem" had at last been licked—whether through the help of expensive psychoanalysis or E.V.'s own summer work programs or a combination of the two. Though E.V. never asked Ed if he'd been cured, he did seem to be rewarding Ed in many ways this summer of 1958 for a job well done. There was no summer "work program" this year, for one thing, and Ed was given a job running an addressograph machine in E.V.'s office at a "damn good salary." E.V. also gave Ed the use of one of his company cars, a new blue and white Ford.

But though Ed may have outwardly given the impression he had reformed, he continued to hire hustlers and was in fact twice *robbed* by hustlers during this summer. The first robbery was set in motion when Ed, driving back to Cincinnati from Walloon Lake in the company car, stopped to pick up a handsome hitchhiker. "I took him to a little hotel that I paid for that was in the Fountain Square area. There, after we had sex, he said he wanted me to live with him but I was very cold and said, 'No.' So then he decided to rob me." Ed willingly handed over his money, asking only that he be allowed to keep the class ring he had just received at his Cranbrook graduation. Although the hustler briefly toyed with the idea of beating him up, Ed escaped unharmed and also managed to keep his class ring. Nonetheless, it had been a harrowing experience, so much so that from that point on Ed was careful to pretend he welcomed any suggestion, no matter how loony, made after sex by the rough trade he picked up.

Yet despite this new wisdom he was robbed a second time when, again driving his father's company car, he picked up a hustler by the bus station in Cincinnati who suggested they park by Fountain Square. Although the hustler claimed that this particular parking place would allow them some privacy, it was actually part of a plan he had worked out beforehand with a partner. Soon after Ed—still sitting in the driver's seat—began giving the hustler fellatio, the driver's door was suddenly swung open by a man holding a knife. The two men took all Ed's money, though Ed again managed to come away unharmed.

There were also other less dangerous if no less bold encounters with men he picked up this summer. During the course of his cruising in downtown Cincinnati Ed had befriended two gay men in their early twenties who talked him into picking up men at the bus station ("there was always this kind of riffraff hanging around there") and then bringing his pickups to a men's toilet in the basement of a nearby church. Ed's two friends would have hidden themselves in the meantime behind an airshaft in the men's room through whose open windows they could watch while Ed "would play with these guys and suck them and carry on." The two grateful voyeurs regarded Ed as "the wildest boy" they had ever met—certainly the best at providing them with "action."

This remarkably precocious sexual boldness, which Ed practiced despite intense guilt, brushes with physical danger, and the paradox of his own penis rarely being involved, is something he felt so "driven" to do that "it was like being self-hypnotized." But bold as Ed may have been, the sex he had was nonetheless furtive, underground sex that took place in a guilt-ridden, sometimes seamy or even dangerous world. It was something he *descended* to (no wonder that in his nightmare about being labeled a homosexual, the realm of homosexuality is pictured as being a dirty, criminal netherworld located below the elegant world of heterosexuality). Furthermore, by turning to homosexual encounters on the heels of having seen his dreams of social acceptance, even social eminence, once again come to nothing, Ed was simply repeating a cycle he had gone through three years earlier when Sally's rejection had set in motion a round of homosexual adventures.

As it turned out, however, this summer between high school and college was the end of an era. The following fall, at the University of Michigan, Ed's conception of what it meant to be homosexual underwent a drastic expansion, embracing for the first time the notion of a gay culture—homosexuality, that is, as something that also encompassed a sensibility, a way of life, and not merely a mode of sex. For if the gay people Ed had known until now had been restricted to hustlers, older bohemians, and anonymous married men, at college he would meet for the first time people his own age and class who were also gay. The summer of 1958 thus marked the end of his life in a predominantly heterosexual world. From this point on Ed would live wholly or partially within a gay subculture, though it would not be until several years after Stonewall that Ed would finally make peace within himself about his homosexuality.

Afterword

I'm often struck today by how many of the fundamental qualities developed in his boyhood remain undiminished in Ed. He's still capable, in his sixties, of bragging with boyish enthusiasm about a new friend or a new sexual conquest he's made, and he still benefits from his occasional boldness ("You'd be surprised what you can get away with"). For all his literary success, there are still times when he sounds as self-doubting and hungry for praise as a young writer just starting out. And though he's been everywhere and done everything, he continues to act like someone who feels he must earn his place among people anew each day by winning everyone over. He still has his capacity for conducting life on a large scale and on many levels at once—social, sexual, artistic, intellectual—and perhaps because he was so divided in himself when he was a kid, so weighed down, he seems today to embody some of the more lighthearted things about the young: their risky openness, their flighty interest in the new, and their unstoppable drive to keep growing.

A Boy's Own Story has found the widest readership of all his books, Ed once told me, because youth is more "universal" than adulthood. I could see his point. Adult lives splinter off, resolving themselves this way or that, but youth remains the primal journey we all take when, haloed by innocence, we feel the thrill of potential even as we're bumping up against the brute facts of life. Perhaps part of the fascination of Edmund White's youth is that upon this elemental landscape of parents and schools and puberty we get to watch a highly original sensibility trying to find its way.

Excerpts

Nocturnes for the King of Naples: pages 69-70.

A Boy's Own Story: pages 8-9, 10, 19-20, 39, 40, 47, 73-76, 80, 92, 106, 107-108, 127, 148, 151, 152.

States of Desire: pages 72, 88.

Forgetting Elena: page 121.

Skinned Alive: Stories: pages 81, 83-84, 87, 113, 129, 139.

The Beautiful Room Is Empty: pages 95, 96, 98, 122.